# Conquering the Content

Jossey-Bass Guides to Online Teaching and Learning

# Conquering
# the Content

## A Blueprint for Online Course Design and Development

SECOND EDITION

Robin M. Smith

**JB JOSSEY-BASS™**
A Wiley Brand

Cover image: © -Vladimir- | Thinkstock

Cover design: Wiley

Published by Jossey-Bass
A Wiley Brand
One Montgomery Street, Suite 1200, San Francisco, CA 94104-4594—www.josseybass.com/highereducation

Jossey-Bass books and products are available through most bookstores. To contact Jossey-Bass directly call our Customer Care Department within the U.S. at 800-956-7739, outside the U.S. at 317-572-3986, or fax 317-572-4002.

Wiley publishes in a variety of print and electronic formats and by print-on-demand. Some material included with standard print versions of this book may not be included in e-books or in print-on-demand. If this book refers to media such as a CD or DVD that is not included in the version you purchased, you may download this material at **http://booksupport.wiley.com**. For more information about Wiley products, visit **www.wiley.com**.

Library of Congress Cataloging-in-Publication Data

Smith, Robin M., 1962-
 Conquering the content : a blueprint for online course design and development /
Robin M. Smith. — Second edition.
  pages cm — (Jossey-bass guides to online teaching and learning)
Includes bibliographical references and index.
 ISBN 978-1-118-71708-0 (paperback)
 ISBN 978-1-118-71710-3 (ebk.)
 ISBN 978-1-118-71714-1 (ebk.)
 1. Web-based instruction—Design. 2. College teaching. I. Title.
 LB1044.87.S617 2014
 378.1'7344678—dc23
                                                                          2014013588

Printed in the United States of America
SECOND EDITION
*PB Printing* 10 9 8 7 6 5 4 3 2 1

# CONTENTS

*Soli Deo Gloria!*

# PREFACE

developed an online biology course with the laboratory in 1997, which was an exciting new experience for me. However, until the course began, I didn't fully comprehend what it might mean to my students. This realization is what changed my career from that of a faculty member teaching in the life sciences to an instructional designer, workshop facilitator, and administrator committed to making higher education accessible to students within their current life situation.

This experience during my first semester teaching online changed my career. Perhaps you've encountered similar students. The names have been changed.

> Steven and his wife, Jenny, have three children: Drew, age five; Seth, three; and Jessica, eighteen months. Steven, a police officer for the local police department, doesn't earn enough at his job to make ends meet for their growing family. The city has tried to increase police salaries, but voters have rejected the last three tax initiatives. Steven took on an additional job just over two years ago when they found out their third child was on the way.

> Steven and Jenny decided they both needed an education to improve their financial situation. Jenny is now in school full-time; with three preschool children, she doesn't work outside the home. Steven took a third job, this one part-time, to help pay for their tuition. Steven will get a raise when he completes his associate's degree, which will allow them to afford the gas for him to commute to the university, forty miles away, one night a week. At the university he can eventually earn a four-year degree, leading to a better, higher-paying job in the police department that will support his family and allow them more stability. There is one problem: the

only class he needs to graduate with his associate's degree is biological sciences with a laboratory; it meets five hours per week over four different days, and there is no way he can juggle all of his work schedules to be off that many hours each week. So far, an entire semester and a summer have elapsed with no solution to this scheduling challenge.

As providence would have it, that fall my biology course was offered online for the first time. Steven was in my course and faithfully logged in every night after his shift ended at 11:00 p.m. Finally, the opportunity to complete an associate's degree, get that raise, and begin work on a bachelor's degree was within reach for Steven! What an amazing opportunity this was for me to understand how important online learning can be in the lives of students.

I have had the good fortune to be connected with countless students for whom online learning has had a life-changing impact. These students have been able to earn a degree from home rather than commute, which has allowed them to get an education that otherwise would have been impossible because of family responsibilities. I live in a rural state, where many individuals need to care for children or aging parents (or both), and may not have transportation reliable enough for a long commute. Online learning is making a positive economic impact on families by allowing individuals to create a better life for themselves and their children. The number of hurdles students—particularly first-generation college students—must jump in order to obtain an education is staggering. Those of us who choose to put our courses online can be part of the solution.

Many of us entered teaching in order to make a difference in people's lives. I have seen the enormous difference online courses can make both to the students who are taking the courses and to their families. Students need options for furthering their education without the constraints of attending face-to-face courses.

I also understand the time constraints faculty have to deal with and the time investment required to develop an online course. With faculty under pressure from so many responsibilities other than teaching, I realized that creating online courses needed to be made less burdensome for faculty.

In order for students to have plentiful opportunities for online learning, it is essential for faculty to have an easy-to-implement method of developing online courses. *Conquering the Content: A Blueprint for Online Course Design and Development* will provide you with a customizable method of developing an online course that is well organized, high quality, and easy to update. It is my goal that with *Conquering the Content* you will create a solid foundation for a course that you can modify as technology changes, your skill level increases, and your experience with online teaching progresses.

The course development system presented in this book is based on educational principles, adult learning principles, online learning principles, and brain and learning theory. It is not subject matter specific, nor is it learning management system specific. Regardless of the subject you are teaching or the way you are delivering your content, the principles in this book are applicable. Using this system also improved my face-to-face teaching, so even if you are not teaching online, your students can benefit from *Conquering the Content*.

An additional goal of *Conquering the Content* is to allow you to remain the subject matter expert. Therefore, I will give you enough information to understand how learning takes place, how teaching online is different from teaching in the face-to-face environment, and what you need to do to get your course online; I also provide information about course design and organization and how to avoid some of the common pitfalls you are likely to encounter as you proceed through the course development process. This book presents a practical approach that will lead you through the lessons. *Conquering the Content* accommodates the flexibility needed to customize your course to fit your own style.

*Conquering the Content* encourages you to look at your course as a whole, select the highest-priority topics for the overall course, and place those items online first. In this way, the fundamentals for the entire course will be established and produced prior to adding anything fancy or flashy to any one chapter or lesson. You'll see later that I recommend using the term *lesson* as opposed to *chapter* because book chapters are likely to change with a new edition, and I'd like to be sure you don't have to make substantial changes each time the book edition changes. Throughout *Conquering the Content,* I have modeled many of the features of course design that I recommend you use in your online course. Therefore, I refer to chapters in this book as lessons; this will also accommodate those students in instructional design courses using *Conquering the Content* as a textbook.

You may not have an award-winning Lesson 1, but you will have completed the basis of the entire course. As an online instructor, I've found the latter to be much preferable to the former. *Conquering the Content* provides the option to add layers to your course as your skills and experience grow. Later you may have that award-winning course, but you probably also will have some online teaching experience to make the revisions you'll need for that award.

Since *Conquering the Content* was published in 2008, I've heard from individuals in a wide variety of settings who have successfully used this system of course development. This process has already proven successful for biological and physical sciences, humanities, history, composition, literature, psychology, philosophy, speech, technical writing, elementary education, mathematics, computer science, accounting, gerontology, wastewater treatment, sleep deprivation, ethics, psychiatry, communications, pharmacy, engineering, health sciences, nursing, education, counseling, business, and numerous other courses. *Conquering the Content* has been adopted at several institutions as their faculty development model for faculty who will be teaching online and is also used as a textbook in multiple instructional design courses.

I'd like to think that every online course has ample development time, a graphic artist, an instructional designer, an animation developer, a peer-review team, a production staff, a pilot test with learners, and time for redevelopment following those activities. However, many of us are essentially on our own to design, develop, and produce our online courses. So we do indeed have some challenges to conquer.

I am confident that you will save time and have a well-structured online course by working through the action steps in this book. Thank you for giving me the opportunity to present these ideas to you.

# THE AUTHOR

Robin M. Smith, Ph.D., is the Director of eLearning at the University of Arkansas at Little Rock, where she leads the accelerated and online programs. Robin has worked at various institutions of higher education and served on numerous grants and federal contracts where she has had the opportunity to quickly launch multiple e-learning programs. Her knowledge of instructional design, adult learning, faculty development, and efficiency of processes has benefited numerous groups with whom she has served as a consultant. Robin holds a Ph.D. in systematic entomology from Texas A&M University. The principles of systematics, taxonomy, and knowledge management apply equally well to insects and course content. Robin has worked with e-learning since 1997 and was one of the first to put a laboratory course online.

Robin enjoys leading practical, results-oriented workshops and may be reached at robinmsmithphd@gmail.com. Her website is http://Conquer ingtheContent.com.

# ACKNOWLEDGMENTS

Thank you to the many workshop participants who have provided feedback and helped refine my ideas and techniques over the years. Those experiences led me to the opportunity to write. I thank Keith Pratt for prompting me to write the first edition of *Conquering the Content* after hearing me speak on chunking course content. It is because of his early vision that you are reading this.

Many thanks to the readers of the first edition who contacted me about their successes with the processes and tools contained in *Conquering the Content: A Step-by-Step Guide to Online Course Design*.

Thank you to the institutions, large and small, who reached out to me after *Conquering the Content* was published, inviting me to travel (in person or virtually) to your campus and conduct workshops to help faculty move forward with development of online courses. I have thoroughly enjoyed the opportunity to meet faculty in person and learn more about online initiatives at institutions where I've been invited to do workshops. Your feedback has contributed to this second edition.

Thank you to those individuals who published reviews of the first edition in scholarly journals. I appreciate your sharing your thoughts with others who may be interested in *Conquering the Content*.

Thank you to Cynthia Saylors, M.Ed., and Katy Warren, M.Ed., for willingly sharing our working example of the Content Map from their online dental radiography course.

Thank you to the anonymous reviewers for providing valuable suggestions and feedback on early drafts. The published version is much stronger because of the time you invested.

My editor, Alison Knowles, has truly partnered with me on *Conquering the Content: A Blueprint for Online Course Design and Development*. Her regular calls and supportive conversations have been invaluable in writing the second edition. I particularly appreciate Alison for catching and sharing my vision of a more graphical layout and for her many efforts to see those ideas through to publication. The second edition is more aesthetically appealing because of her.

Many thanks to my family, friends, and colleagues for their patience, support, and encouragement throughout the process of moving the ideas from my mind into publishable form!

# INTRODUCTION

Much of the format of *Conquering the Content: A Blueprint for Online Course Design and Development* serves as a model of the suggestions I present for each of the lessons in your online course. Just as I have used this development system to create both online and face-to-face courses, I also used it to develop and organize the content for this book. I believe you will find that *Conquering the Content* presents an organized approach to design and development of online courses that you will also find useful for face-to-face courses.

Each of my online courses has a **Begin Here** segment that describes the way the course will work and essential elements such as the syllabus, schedule, and other course overview documents that learners will need to gain an understanding of how to proceed through the course. In addition, background information for the course content is in this section. Lesson 1 serves that purpose in this book.

In my online courses as well as in *Conquering the Content*, I begin each lesson with a **Content Map.** The Content Map presents an overview of the topics, presents information retrieval cues to learners, and provides context by illustrating the placement of a topic within the remainder of the content. In Lesson 2, we will develop the Content Map for your online course.

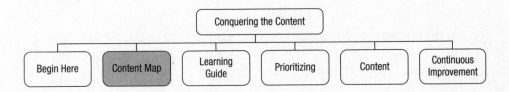

 PLAY AUDIO INTRODUCTION The second component is the **lesson introduction,** which is typically an audio or video segment introducing the topic. I had an outpouring of positive feedback from learners when I added this feature to my online course. Giving an opportunity for learners to hear directly from me helps them feel connected and confident that they understand my directions. This feature of the course represents Mayer's Personalization Theory and supports the theoretical rationale of that theory by speaking directly to the learners (Mayer, 2009). **Lesson Relevance:** I also include a **lesson relevance** statement to provide an overview of each lesson and highlight why it matters. Making the learning relevant helps students connect new content to their prior learning; it also helps with student motivation. If students do not find the content of the course interesting or relevant, they may see little or no value in mastering it and may fail to engage in the behaviors required for deep learning (Ambrose et al., 2010).

The next major feature of the course and this book is the **Learning Guide,** which serves three major purposes. The Learning Guide is developed early in the process of *Conquering the Content* and will serve as a course development map for the remainder of your content. It is also your key to an easily updateable course. In addition, the Learning Guide is a one-page overview of the lesson, which learners will typically print out to use whether they are studying content online or offline. The Learning Guide has widespread impact on both you and your students, so we will take extra time to ensure that this critical feature provides a very stable foundation for your online course. Lesson 3 will highlight the many benefits of the Learning Guide and guide you through development of your own.

Once the Content Map and Learning Guides have been established, we will spend time in Lesson 4, **Prioritizing.** It is essential that we determine the features of your online course to develop first. Throughout *Conquering the Content,* we focus on ensuring that you develop the course in stages so that you begin with a foundation of the entire course before adding layers of richness. There are several reasons for this, not the least of which is that I am very cognizant of your time constraints. I know that you may have to

## LEARNING OBJECTIVES

| Prioritizing | Upon completion of this lesson, you will be able to: |
|---|---|
| | • Rank in priority order the features of your online course to develop. |
| | • Plan sequential improvements to your online course. |
| | • Add layers of richness to your course as time permits. |

## LEARNING RESOURCES

| References | • Smith, R. "Lesson 3, Learning Guides." *Conquering the Content: A Blueprint for Online Course Design and Development*. San Francisco: Jossey-Bass, 2014. |
|---|---|
| | • Learning Guides developed in Lesson 3. |

## Content

| Required Resource | • Smith, R. "Lesson 4, Prioritizing." *Conquering the Content: A Blueprint for Online Course Design and Development*. San Francisco: Jossey-Bass, 2014. |
|---|---|

## LEARNING ACTIVITIES

| Activities for This Lesson | • Rank in priority order the yet to be developed features of your course that will have the greatest impact for learners. |
|---|---|
| | • Rank from shortest to longest the yet to be developed features of your course based on your best guess about how long it will take to complete these portions. |
| | • Plot the learner impact and development time of the remaining items in the course. |
| | • Prioritize the most important features of the course to place online first. |

## Self-Assessment

| Check Your Understanding | • Selection of the course features with the highest impact on learners. |
|---|---|
| | • Selection of the least time-consuming features of the course. |

## Lesson Assessment

| "Graded" Assessments or Evidence to Proceed | • Prioritized list of the features to develop |
|---|---|

stop before you are completely finished with the course, and with this system, that is OK! My goal is to help you through course development as far as you possibly can get before you run out of time, but I know that at some point you will likely run out of time. Following this system, we will ensure that you have multiple points along the development path that provide an option to stop developing and begin delivering the course. You will have established a firm foundation for your entire course by the end of Lesson 3. Each subsequent lesson adds layers of richness to the entire course.

Once you have established priorities for course development, we will move to Lesson 5, **Content,** where we will focus on the presentation of your subject matter. Because most of the content for this book is text based, the modeling is not quite as rich in this lesson as it could be in another format. By placing your content online, you will have many more options than those I am able to model in a book format. We will focus on aspects of working memory, learning principles, chunking, and the appropriate way to present content in the online environment. I hope you will take advantage of the many options available online for presenting content. This is where the advantages of online learning really shine.

Throughout *Conquering the Content,* I intersperse **Action Items.** These are similar to the Learning Activities in your online course. As highlighted in Lesson 5, Content, presenting some content and then asking learners to participate in an activity helps reinforce their learning and will provide opportunities for feedback about how well they are grasping the concepts.

**ACTION ITEM 10**

Using the outline you created, add topics to the Content Map format of your choice.

Also interspersed throughout the book are time-saving tips to help you be efficient with your online courses.

 **TIME-SAVING TIP**

Overall course structure should be independent of time and of book chapters.

In Lesson 6, **Continuous Improvement,** I will highlight some best practices for course delivery and also some convenient and efficient methods for capturing and incorporating updates to your course each time you teach it.

At the end of each lesson, I include two items to help share ideas. One is "Conquering the Content in Action," in which I describe successes other faculty members have experienced using the *Conquering the Content* system.

I also invite you to connect with the online *Conquering the Content* Community by using the links associated with the "Share" image so that you can share examples from your course as well as view examples from others.

## FACULTY EXPERIENCES WITH PRIORITIZING AND LAYERING

- A faculty member uncertain about teaching online used layering to gradually increase portions of his course that were online so that the online component advanced from supplemental to fully online. Positive learner feedback and allowing himself time to become more comfortable with the online environment were the keys to success.

- A reluctant humanities professor became interested and motivated to move additional components of the course to the online environment when an opportunity for international travel arose during the semester.

- An elementary education professor is using prioritizing and layering to help future teachers learn to teach online.

Share your Begin Here ideas and view others in the *Conquering the Content* Community: http://ConqueringtheContent.com/BH/Share

Now that you've had an overview of how the book guides you through the design and development process, I believe that together we can conquer the content in your online course!

# Conquering the Content

# 1

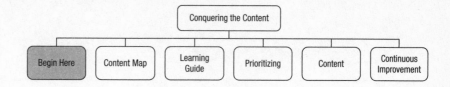

Conquering the Content

| Begin Here | Content Map | Learning Guide | Prioritizing | Content | Continuous Improvement |

# BEGIN HERE

PLAY AUDIO
INTRODUCTION  HTTP://CONQUERINGTHECONTENT.COM/BH/INTRO

**Lesson Relevance:** This lesson will set the stage for development of your online course. We will highlight some of the differences between the face-to-face and online environments, recognize that it is natural to feel uncomfortable when making these alterations to your teaching, highlight the importance of separating course development from course delivery, prepare for future updates to your course, and answer some typical questions of first-time online instructors.

## CONQUERING THE CONTENT: A BLUEPRINT FOR ONLINE COURSE DESIGN AND DEVELOPMENT

Lesson 1, Begin Here

## LEARNING GOALS/OUTCOMES

Begin Here

Upon completion of this lesson, you will be able to:

- Infer qualities of good teachers by describing a teacher who positively influenced you.
- Explain the value that you, as a unique individual, bring to your subject matter.
- Differentiate between the environments of online and face-to-face courses.
- Separate design and development tasks from delivery tasks.
- Recognize the need to design with updating in mind.
- Resolve some issues of first-time online instructors.
- Begin to approach course design from the learner's perspective.
- Document current course organization and structure.

## LEARNING RESOURCES

References

- Chickering, A., and Gamson, Z. "Seven Principles for Good Practice in Undergraduate Education." *AAHE Bulletin,* Mar. 1987, pp. 3–6.
- Felder, R. "Learning and Teaching Styles in Engineering Education." *Engineering Education,* 1988, *78*(7), 674–681.
- Merrill, M. "First Principles of Instruction." *Educational Technology Research and Development,* 2002, *50*(3), 43–59.

## CONTENT

Required Resource

- Smith, R. "Lesson 1, Begin Here." *Conquering the Content: A Blueprint for Online Course Design and Development.* San Francisco: Jossey-Bass, 2014.

## LEARNING ACTIVITIES

Activities for This Lesson

- Describe your favorite teacher.
- Identify the value you, as a unique individual, add to a course.
- Select one course on which to work.
- Gather materials for the course that you will place online.
- Identify improvements needed for your current course.

## SELF-ASSESSMENT

Check Your Understanding

- Express qualities important for good teaching.
- Switch your perspective from teaching to learning.
- Recognize the added value you bring to your learners.

## LESSON ASSESSMENT

"Graded" Assessments or Evidence to Proceed

- Materials needed to develop course
- Course improvement ideas

# GOOD TEACHING

Why are you involved in education? Who influenced you to invest part of your life's work in teaching and learning? Is there any particular person who stands out to you as someone who helped shape your decision to be involved in education? As faculty members we usually choose our subject matter because of passion for that topic. The natural world and problem solving intrigue me; therefore, I originally trained as a scientist. What is it that made you select your discipline? Perhaps it was a teacher who took a special interest in you, a class that challenged you, or some particular lesson that touched you at a sensitive time in your life. Typically, a person's favorite teacher is not one who was his or her easiest teacher; rather the person provided motivation, inspiration, practical application, or something similar. Your learners will likely find these qualities beneficial as well.

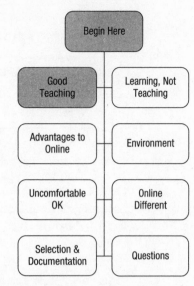

## ACTION ITEM 1

Think of your favorite teacher from all your years of school—the one who made a positive lasting impression on you.

Using Form 1, document the qualities that stood out about this person.

## MY FAVORITE TEACHER

| QUESTIONS | RESPONSES |
|---|---|
| Subject this person taught | |
| The year in school I had this teacher | |
| The main thing that comes to mind when I think of this teacher | |
| What he or she did that caught my attention | |
| The qualities that stand out about his or her teaching | |
| What I'd like to adopt from this person | |

Form available at www.josseybass.com/go/conqueringthecontent

In addition to learning effective practices from those who taught us, we can adopt the teaching principles found to be the most effective, which have been documented by several studies.

You may be familiar with the classic study by Chickering and Gamson (1987), which established seven principles for undergraduate teaching:

- Encourage faculty-to-learner interaction.
- Encourage learner-to-learner interaction.
- Promote active learning.
- Communicate high expectations.
- Facilitate time on task.
- Provide rich, rapid feedback.
- Respect diverse learning.

These same teaching principles hold true whether you are teaching in a face-to-face or an online environment. If you are not familiar with these principles,

I encourage you to find and review this study. Among the many additional articles referencing Chickering and Gamson's original work is Chickering and Ehrmann's "Implementing the Seven Principles: Technology as Lever" (1996), which provides ideas for using the seven principles in an online course.

Another excellent guide for online courses is Merrill's "First Principles of Instruction" (2002). Most effective learning environments are those that are problem based and involve learners in four distinct phases of learning:

- Activation of prior experience
- Demonstration of skills
- Application of skills
- Integration of these skills into real-world activities

These principles can be applied to instructional design; learning is facilitated when

- Learners are engaged in solving real-world problems.
- Existing knowledge is activated as a foundation for new knowledge.
- New knowledge is demonstrated to the learner.
- It is applied by the learner.
- It is integrated into the learner's world.

No one would expect an athlete or a musician to perform without hours of practice. Yet much instruction seems to assume that when it comes to cognitive skills, such practice is unnecessary. Merrill (2002) notes that "appropriate practice is the single most neglected aspect of effective instruction" (p. 43).

Your learning experience, research, and your own teaching experience work together to help inform your teaching. It is important to identify the unique contributions you bring to course delivery in the face-to-face environment so that we do not miss the opportunity to incorporate those into your online course. I'm providing some structures for you to use in your online course, and these will be very helpful, but if you incorporate every structural element described in *Conquering the Content* but do not include your unique contributions, your learners will be missing out.

What is it that learners can learn from you that they cannot get from any other source (book, journal article, another teacher)? Whatever you identify here is *highly* important to communicate in your online course. Perhaps it is the way you think through and solve problems, the way you can add humor to the topic, how you've learned to remember important portions of the content, your experiences applying course concepts, or any number of other things that might be distinctive to you. This is what makes you a unique teacher with an important contribution to your learners; we don't want this to be absent from your online course!

ACTION ITEM 2

Brainstorm for a few minutes about the added value you as a unique individual bring to your course.

FORM 2

## MY ADDED VALUE

| QUESTIONS | RESPONSES |
|---|---|
| What are some of your unique characteristics that learners benefit from by having you as their instructor? | |
| What can learners get from you that they cannot get from any other source (book, journal article, Internet, another teacher)? | |
| How do you think through scenarios or problem-solve that learners would benefit from understanding? | |
| What about your teaching do students positively comment on? | |
| What unique experiences do you have that give you insight into your subject matter? | |

Form available at www.josseybass.com/go/conqueringthecontent

# THINK LEARNING, NOT TEACHING

We typically think of our courses as what we will teach. Instead, if you alter your perspective to that of the learners in your course and think, "What do participants need to learn?" you will facilitate the design process tremendously.

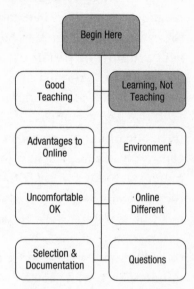

Just as you want only enough information to put your course online, detailed steps about how to do the things you need to do, and hints about pitfalls to avoid—all without a bunch of extraneous explanation or background information—your learners want the same kinds of things. Think about how you proceed when you go to the Internet to look up information. You likely search to find

- The best match for the subject at hand. You probably don't want to read thirty articles. Instead you'd like to find just a few of the facts you need, presented clearly.

- Quick-loading information. If you have to wait more than five or ten seconds for a page to load, you might abandon that site for a different one.

- Clear, precise information with images to confirm you have identified things appropriately or are correctly going about the steps to a new task.

- Checks or verifications along the way in a project so that you don't get to the end of a sixteen-step process and find out you did something wrong in step 2. You want to know on step 2 whether you are right before proceeding to step 3.

- Few to no time wasters, which are frustrating and preventable.

Learners in your online course will be looking for similar things from you. Learning online is very different from learning in the face-to-face environment; therefore, using exactly what has worked for teaching materials in the past is not going to be suitable for online teaching. This is a rather tough adjustment for most faculty. We usually teach as we were taught, and those teachers taught us the way they had been taught, and so the cycle has gone for many decades or centuries. As Tony Bates, a prominent authority on distance learning points out, "to change is more work. You've got to be trained; you've got to learn new things; you've got to do things that you've never done before" (Awalt, 2007, p. 107).

Today we have powerful tools that have altered the learning environment and offer opportunities to work in new ways. In addition, we are constantly discovering new information about learning and brain research. Moreover, today's learners have grown up in a visual environment, and they typically process multiple inputs at one time. They may simultaneously be searching the Internet, text messaging, listening to music, and talking on the phone. Then we wonder why they can't pay attention when they sit in our course and we lecture to (at?) them continuously for fifty minutes. Even television shows are incorporating the option of commenting during the airing of the show, with the comments visible to viewers. This creates an active conversation around the content, which offers a richer experience for viewers. Perhaps we can learn from this example and offer similar options to our students.

## Learner-Centered Environment

One of the major advantages to having course materials available online is that it allows repetition of content for those learners who need more than one time through the content to grasp the material. Who said that a degree should be available only to those learners who can "get it" the first time through the content? If learners need to repeat the content seven times to fully comprehend it, and are willing to take the time to go through it seven times, shouldn't they also have the opportunity for credit?

The learner-centered environment of an online course has a number of facets:

- **Self-selected.** That learners choose when to come into the course and work on the subject matter adds a distinct psychological advantage: they are mentally prepared because they chose to work on the course materials. Even if it's to avoid something else they don't want to do (laundry, working in someone else's course), they've *chosen* to come to class. In contrast, in a face-to-face course, the learners are required to attend at a specific time. Even if they originally selected this schedule themselves, a given Wednesday at 10:00 a.m. may not be a suitable time for learning, for any number of reasons. By the way, you as a faculty member also get to self-select the moment you go to class in an online course. This can very beneficial to your schedule as well.

- **Time.** Learners may work at the time of day when they are at their best. You may be at your best in the morning; if so, you can develop your course materials in the mornings. Some learners may be at their best at 11:00 p.m. and "come to class" then. Another learner can "come to class" at 2:00 a.m. With everyone working at his or her optimum time of the day, both the course and the participation in the course are more likely to represent the best effort possible, and we therefore get a better learning experience. With content and other course materials online, this information is available around the clock. So even if you are not placing your entire course online, you can provide some online features to aid learners.

- **Place.** Learners can choose a place where they can concentrate well and at their convenience. A learner who is traveling for work or vacation is able to participate in the learning activities regardless of his or her location. This means that learners can keep up with course work much more conveniently than learners limited to the face-to-face environment, who if they have a conflict at, say, 10:00 on Monday, totally miss whatever happens in class. In an online course, the option is still there for learners to get the content even though 10:00 on Monday did not work for them. Many face-to-face instructors are taking advantage of online submission of work. This offers many advantages, including ease of assignment submission, a record of submission, ease of grading, and return of work to learners.

- **Pace.** Online learners can move quickly through content they understand, go slowly through content they do not understand, and repeat sections as needed. Faculty members have always had the difficulty of not reaching all learners. Some learners are left behind, while others are not challenged enough. With an online course, learners can take care of this for themselves. And because materials are already online, there is no extra effort required by the faculty member to meet the individual pacing needs of learners.

# Plan for Online from the Beginning

Have you ever had to make a presentation when the equipment was different from what you had been told it would be, or you attended a presentation where the equipment didn't match what the presenter had brought? Maybe the presenter brought materials for a computer and an LCD projector, but the meeting site was prepared for someone with transparencies (previous-century technology). Unless there is a way of transferring information quickly from one format to another or a way to improvise on the fly, the entire exchange of information may be compromised. The same is true if you do not plan your online course as an online course from the beginning. If you've been teaching a face-to-face course for years and show up to an online course with your face-to-face materials, it's like standing in front of a computer and an LCD projector trying to figure out a place from which to transmit your transparencies. There is no such place. Those two modes of communication are not compatible.

In *Learner-Centered Teaching*, Weimer (2002) points out that "the piecemeal addition of new techniques does not transform teaching." Instead, we need to approach change systematically. "Systematic change means change that is planned, prepared, and then implemented according to some process" (p. 185). The course must be planned as an online course from the start. That is why we begin with revisiting goals and learning outcomes in Lesson 1 and brainstorming the best way for learners to achieve those outcomes. With online technology, there are some limitations and freedoms not offered to us when we're teaching by other delivery modes.

# Select Technology Based on Pedagogy

Gratuitous use of technology is not impressive to learners. They've seen much better than what we are able to place into a learning management system (LMS), so using a tool just to use it is not helpful. There should be an educational reason for use of the tools in your course. The course content is to be the challenge of the course, not the use of the technology. If there are tools your learners may be unfamiliar with, providing instructions for how to use them is vital.

It is also important to time the introduction of new tools in such a way that use of the tool doesn't add to the challenge of the assignment. Remember, we want to keep the content front and center and have the technology as invisible and comfortable as possible. Therefore, if you will plan to use a particular tool for learners to submit a high-stakes assignment, it is better to introduce use of that tool earlier in a low-stakes assignment or in an element with few points associated so that students can gain experience with the submissions process.

During one semester, a faculty member I was working with had learned to use a new tool in the LMS, and she was interested in having the learners use that tool to turn in their final paper. We talked about the way the learners had turned in their other papers throughout the semester, which was through the use of a very different submission method. No additional assignments were due prior to the major final paper. My suggestion was that the learners' stress level was going to be rather high for getting their final paper completed anyway, and introducing a new tool to go along with the assignment itself would cause additional, unnecessary stress. She agreed and waited until the next semester to use the newer tool. In that situation, the technology was not going to be an enhancement, and it was not going to be invisible; it was going to be invasive and disruptive to the learning process. Her conclusion was that although it would be much more efficient for her, it was better for the learners not to have to deal with a new tool at that point in the semester.

# ADVANTAGES TO HAVING A COURSE ONLINE

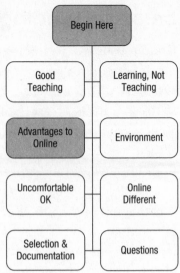

I knew learners would appreciate the convenience of accessing information on their own schedule, the absence of a face-to-face attendance requirement, and the ability to review course content and presentations more than the one time they were presented in the face-to-face environment. However, after my course was online, I realized additional advantages that I had not anticipated. Some of these advantages were due to the advance preparation of the online course, which had to be complete before the semester began. For example:

- Learners can hurry through concepts that are familiar to them and go slower through concepts for which they need additional time.

- The online course provided a solid base from which to update my course because everything was documented, and review and update of content was more convenient.

- Static content enabled the learners to provide more meaningful feedback about those aspects and portions of the content where they needed additional explanation to facilitate better understanding.

- The experience of teaching online enabled me to also increase the organization and structure for my face-to-face courses. Learners in my face-to-face courses noticed an improvement in my teaching as I began teaching online.

- Learners in my face-to-face courses benefited from the Learning Guides that I began providing for them after using them in the online environment.

- I knew for certain what the online learners were viewing as magnified images. When we met in the laboratory, in contrast, I was unable to check with each learner on each microscope image.

- It was much easier for me to critique my own course materials online than to critique a videotape of myself presenting those materials.

- With content online, my focus and that of the learners became the content. Rather than standing between my learners and the content (as it seemed in the face-to-face environment), I was now standing beside my learners, and we were all focusing on the content.

- It was easier to incorporate the suggestions from external reviews, because they could review the course material on their own time. The online materials provided a target for review that was impersonal compared to critiques of my face-to-face presentations. Reviewers found it much more comfortable to provide constructive feedback.

- The switch to teaching online meant that my day was more flexible.

# ENVIRONMENT

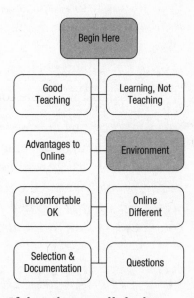

Just as it was best for me to write this book fully accepting the reality that you will not have the opportunity to place your entire course online all at once, it is best for you to develop your course fully accepting that your learners will not have uninterrupted time to work on your online course. It would be ideal if they had a protected hour to work on the course when nothing else was happening, but how many of us have blocks of time with no interruptions? We need to plan our courses with an understanding that learners will have interruptions. If they do not, all the better, but telling them they need to put aside a specific time to work on your course and commit to that time is like expecting learners to have questions for you only during your office hours. We've all experienced the limitations of that plan!

## The Online Learner's Environment

Rather than being surrounded by a room full of other learners who are focused on the same subject matter for a period of time, an online learner may be surrounded by any number of circumstances at home. Crying babies have no concern for class time; if they are in distress, now is the time for action. By the same token, ringing phones, toddlers, meal preparation, carpools, work, and other duties often require that learners interrupt their online learning time. Do not underestimate the distractions that a learner may be dealing with at home. These distractions will be competing with your course content for attention. Environmental factors have a strong impact on learner concentration levels for online courses.

## The Two-Minute Test

I was fortunate to be in the audience recently for a learner panel on online courses. To my surprise, the learners indicated that they make a decision about whether their online course will be a good one or a bad one within the first two minutes of their initial login to the course. The learners indicated that they base this decision on how well the course is organized. It is crucial for your learners' benefit and for your own self-preservation that your course be designed in such a way that it creates a clear pathway of learning through the content. The most frequent criticism I hear about online courses is how confusing the course is or how unclear it is to find the proper path within the course. *Conquering the Content* will provide a strong organizational framework for your course and ensure that your course can pass the Two-Minute Test.

## IT'S OK TO BE UNCOMFORTABLE

Faculty members are experts in their subject matter, and if you have many years of teaching experience, you most likely feel comfortable in the face-to-face environment. Many faculty thrive on the experience of sharing what they know with others. They have become accustomed to sharing their knowledge in a face-to-face setting. If you are suddenly asked to alter those surroundings and place a course online, you may find yourself going through some major adjustments.

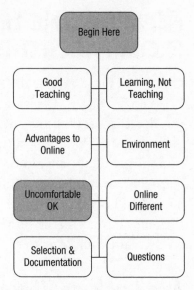

First, rather than being the expert, you find yourself in unfamiliar surroundings. You might think, "I don't know how to put my course online, and I don't have time to put my course online." Put your mind at ease: you are supposed to feel uncomfortable about this and unsure about what you are doing. That is natural the first time you do something. It might feel uncomfortable even for a few semesters. It's OK to do things you've never done before—that's how we learn!

All of us who have put a course online did so the first time not really knowing what we were doing. This discomfort may actually be an advantage, according to Weimer (2002, p. 188): "When we opt for change that is not comfortable and is entirely out of the ordinary for us, we open ourselves to teaching as a learning experience, a point of personal development." You are still going to be the subject matter expert; you may not be the technical expert, but honestly, do you really want to be? It is expected that you will ask for help on technical matters; you are not compromising your expertise.

Of course, you are going to have questions about online learning and the LMS; that is a given. But you don't have time to learn everything there is to know about all of it, so prioritizing the things you need to know in order to teach your course is important. Learn from others who may be ahead of you; most people love to share information. There is likely a support unit at your institution. Find out what resources are available to you as you develop your online course. Is there someone to help with instructional design? Copyright issues? Production? If so, that is wonderful; take advantage of their services. If not, this need not deter you from making your course work available to students who are trying to further their education.

# HOW ONLINE LEARNING IS DIFFERENT FROM FACE-TO-FACE LEARNING

One of the most notable differences between the face-to-face and online environments is just that: the environment. First, you aren't standing at the front of the room ready to dispense knowledge to the learners. Second, they typically are not in a room full of other learners. In addition, they may or may not dedicate fifty minutes solely to the subject matter.

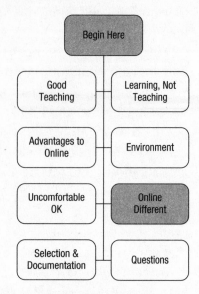

## The Lack of Visual Cues

In the face-to-face environment, when you give encouraging words to one learner, you are simultaneously giving positive feedback to all the learners. But online learners never hear these words to other learners. Nor do they hear you say "good morning" or see a smile from you each class period. None of those cues are available to learners in online courses. Instead, for online learners, everything becomes verbal; it takes lots of verbal positive reinforcement to replace all those visual cues that they are not receiving.

## The Learner's Role

Learners in an online environment are more responsible for their own learning than are those in a face-to-face environment. There is no longer a person standing at the front of the room to guide the learner through a lesson for an hour. Online learners need enough discipline to come to class by logging in and then working through the content. This is placing more responsibility on the learner to begin with. In addition, there is no one there saying, "Class is over at ten to the hour." So learners might continue working longer on a given lesson if their concentration is high (or a deadline is approaching) or might take a break earlier if their concentration is off at that moment.

It is helpful if you point out this greater responsibility to your learners. The Begin Here section of your course would be a great place for this information. Carol Dweck's research (2006) indicates that sharing with learners that they can improve with practice and repeated attempts can make a difference in their learning.

The greater responsibility of learners is another reason that directions and the pathway for progress through the course must be abundantly clear to them. Learning Guides, discussed in Lesson 3, help illuminate this pathway through the course.

Because of these differences in the environment, course content requires the following characteristics:

- Ability to be separated into short, directed learning segments—**chunk-ability**

- Ability to repeat and review content—**repeat-ability**

- Ability to stop and resume without having to start all over—**pause-ability**

- Ability to be easily comprehensible to learners—**understand-ability**

We'll talk more about these features in Lesson 5, Content, as you develop your content presentations.

## The Faculty Member's Role

We've alluded to the changing role of the faculty member and the fact that this may be an adjustment for many individuals. Once you get over the initial shock of not being the one the students are focused on, it can be very freeing to help your learners see the reasons you are passionate about your subject matter. "Let me show you how cool this is!" is a much more invigorating role than "I'm going to teach you this." If you'll jump into this role with both feet, I think you'll be pleased with the results! It is perhaps a subtle change, but nevertheless an important one because it means taking on different responsibilities. You now need to explain the information, explore how to make connections with it, decipher what is most important, explain how it matters to everyday life, and reveal your thinking and problem-solving methods to learners. Your role now is to make sure that you present information in a way that is relevant, understandable, memorable, and useful to the learners.

A faculty member who is acting as the sage on the stage is reaping the benefits of working with, structuring, and communicating the content. One goal in designing effective and efficient learning environments is for learners to work as intensively with the content as we might when teaching. Strategies that support this shift in perspective include having the students moderate discussion forums, prepare concept summaries and examples for other students, and assume greater responsibility as frontline moderators for the course (Boettcher, 2007).

## The Distinction Between Course Design and Development and Course Delivery and Facilitation

This change in faculty role highlights the necessary distinction between design and development activities and delivery and facilitation activities in online courses. Your institution may have a template design that is used for courses in your program or on your campus. This has the added advantage that students are free to focus fully on the content in your course and not have the burden of relearning a different navigation method for each course. You may find yourself developing a course you do not end up teaching, or teaching a course you did not develop. This is becoming more and more common as institutions increase the number of online courses offered. Whether that is your situation or not, design/development and delivery/facilitation are independent, but also highly interdependent, activities in online courses.

Unlike in a face-to-face course, in an online course the course design and development tasks need to be completed before any portion of the course is delivered, so that the semester can be spent on the delivery and facilitation aspects of the course. In this book, we will focus most of our time on course design and development. There are several good references to aid course facilitation, including Conrad and Donaldson (2012), Lehman and Conceição (2010), and Palloff and Pratt (2004).

# The Current Preparation for Future Updates

Most courses need to be updated soon after being produced; therefore, it is best to design your course from the beginning such that it accommodates updates. The course development system described in this book is strategically planned so that the design and organization of content and the placement of certain aspects of the course create a blueprint for the process of design, which also accommodates updating your course in a systematic way.

Perhaps you are now teaching a course that meets only in the fall, and you have no plans to change that schedule. Nevertheless, with the rapidly changing e-learning environment, it is difficult to anticipate exactly what will take place in the next few years. Therefore, by following the blueprint in *Conquering the Content*, you will be ready when the need arises for you to teach the course in a five-week summer term, a four-week midwinter course, a six- or seven-week accelerated course, or any other format that might arise. We will be naming content based on topics rather than time. Also, book and chapter number references will be confined to a particular place (Learning Guides) so that you needn't track down those references throughout the many pages of course information.

In addition, this course design system will prepare you for the new edition of the book you use. As educators, we do not want to place ourselves in the position that our course materials are in such great shape that we do not want to update them or that it's too much trouble to update them. As I created my first online course, I realized how much work I was putting into it and knew I had to make it easy to update; starting from scratch was going to be more than I was prepared to tackle in the near future. Content in this system is named and labeled in a logical and retrievable manner and is in segments short enough that when you need to make changes, you do not have to recreate large portions of the course.

In addition to book and information updates, sometimes a rapid response time is extremely important when updates to content are needed. In a project I was involved with, we needed to release content revisions to medical learners concerning the switch in position on hormone replacement therapy, and to do so quickly. We needed to be able to update the online course in one week. The majority of that time was spent on developing the content; we were able to update the course in minutes. Fortunately, the design of the course allowed the updates to be added easily. Following this design system will allow you to do the same.

This system will also accommodate adding components to the course progressively as you teach. The majority of teachers are constantly monitoring and adjusting, and it is no different in an online course. After you have taught your online course the first time, you will find components you'd like to alter based on your experience and learner feedback. This system makes editing and adding improvements to your course easy.

## COURSE SELECTION AND DOCUMENTATION

Select one course to develop as you work through *Conquering the Content*. You may have more than one you need to complete, but for now, choose only one. Preferably this course will be taught a semester or two in the future so that you will have some time to work through this book. As you recall from the Introduction, there will be stopping points along the way, so regardless of the amount of time you have before you begin teaching this course, we can make excellent progress toward a well-organized course.

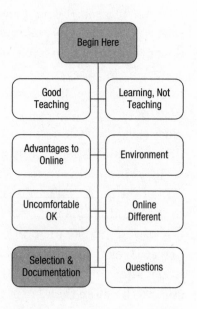

Begin Here

Good Teaching

Learning, Not Teaching

Advantages to Online

Environment

Uncomfortable OK

Online Different

Selection & Documentation

Questions

**ACTION ITEM 3**

Select one course on which to focus as you work through the process outlined in this book.

Gather all materials associated with the selected course, including syllabus, schedule, objectives, assignments, quizzes, book, feedback from student evaluations of teaching, and so on.

# Course Documentation

For now, it will be helpful to document what is currently taking place in the course you'd like to work with as we progress through *Conquering the Content*.

To facilitate understanding, I'm providing a completed example of the next Action Item and form.

## EXCERPT FROM COMPLETED SAMPLE

| CURRENT CONTENT ORGANIZATION | | |
|---|---|---|
| **Content Covered** | **Quiz or Assignment** | **Notes** |
| Ecology | Quiz—100 points | Easy lesson, most students are familiar with the topic |
| Cells | Quiz—100 points | Difficult topic, need lots of visuals |
| Cell Physiology | Process Project—100 points Quiz—50 points | Long lesson, difficult for learners to understand, need some animations or sequential still drawings so learners can grasp concepts. Addition of the project helps learners understand the one process they produce; how to help them with the others? Possibly add learner presentations so others can benefit from their work. |

Document current course organization and the benefits or challenges of individual lessons.

FORM 5

## CURRENT COURSE ORGANIZATION

| CURRENT CONTENT ORGANIZATION | | |
| --- | --- | --- |
| Content Covered | Quiz or Assignment | Notes |
| | | |
| | | |
| | | |
| | | |
| | | |

Form available at www.josseybass.com/go/conqueringthecontent

# QUESTIONS FROM FIRST-TIME ONLINE INSTRUCTORS

I typically am asked the same several questions each time a new instructor begins teaching online. I'll answer those for you here. If you have taught online before, you might quickly skim over these questions and take this opportunity to save a bit of time and move ahead to Lesson 2, Content Map.

| | |
|---|---|
| Begin Here | |
| Good Teaching | Learning, Not Teaching |
| Advantages to Online | Environment |
| Uncomfortable OK | Online Different |
| Selection & Documentation | Questions |

## How Do I Know It's the Learner Doing the Work?

One thing you can do is to have learners turn in intermediate steps to the assignments so that you can learn the character and quality of their writing and work. For example, if learners have to write a term paper, you might require that they turn in the following items at progressive dates along the way to the final paper:

- Topic
- Resources to use
- Draft outline
- Revised outline
- Two to three draft paragraphs and additional subpoints for other sections of the outline
- Three to six draft paragraphs and additional subpoints for the remainder of the outline
- Bibliography
- A rough draft of the paper
- The final rewritten paper, including the bibliography

With all of these steps, the learner will have to show you work along the way. You can do the same thing for a speech, oral presentation, or lab project by asking to see all the intermediate steps. This also enables you to give feedback to the learners. It helps them understand the development process for a major project, assists them with pacing themselves, and typically leads to their ending up with a much better final product than if they had not had to turn in these intermediate products for review.

## How Do I Know It's the Learner Taking the Test?

Unless you have the learners use a webcam (and you watch each one individually), you really do not know that the correct learner is taking the text. In fact, the same situation exists in classes with large numbers of learners: you do not know that the correct learners are taking the test unless you check identification cards as they enter the room. Another option some faculty select is to have the learners go to a testing center for their exams, where they must present their identification. However, relying totally on exams for grades is not a recommended practice. Project-based assignments and other authentic assessments are more valuable.

## How Do I Know They Aren't Looking at Their Books During the Test?

Unless you have them in a monitored environment, you don't. You just assume that they are looking at their books. Therefore, ask questions about concepts and ideas, not sentences from the book.

In a freshman biology course, I actually told my learners to have their books, notes, study guide, and everything else they'd done for class all filled out right in front of them for the test. This policy encouraged them to do the exercises I'd assigned. It did not punish those honest individuals who if I had said "no books" would have had "no books," while everyone else in the class would have had their books in front of them and thought nothing of it. Except to clarify spelling or some small point, the books and other study aids were of little help (and I had told them this in advance). I was testing concepts and ideas, and asking them to apply these concepts and ideas. I was not lifting sentences out of the book and making multiple-choice questions out of them.

# How Do I Balance Effort and Points?

You are trading one commodity for another with the learners. The commodity you have to trade is points; the commodity the learners have to trade is time and effort. Therefore, if an assignment takes a large amount of time and effort, it should be rewarded with a large number of points in your course. Conversely, if an assignment or test requires a small effort and little time, it should earn a small number of points in your course. I know that this is mostly common sense, but sometimes it is helpful to state the obvious. I had students complain once that a faculty member had only 10 points in the entire course. A three-page paper was worth one point. I know that is the same as 100 points out of 1,000, but it was disorienting to students compared to the amount of points they received for similar effort in other courses. If you want learners to spend a lot of time on an assignment, you signal that by the number of points you attach to it.

# How Do I See the Lightbulb Turning On or the Blank Stare?

It is essential that you incorporate enough feedback and response opportunities from learners so that you will know how things are going. Rather than being able to look into their eyes, you will now be using their work, the questions, and their conversations as your gauge for how learners are progressing with their understanding. In the face-to-face environment, you have daily opportunities to read their reactions; if you use only the major tests to gauge their understanding, you will miss opportunities to correct misperceptions, reteach portions of the course, and clarify difficult concepts.

# How Can I Teach Online and Still Have a Balanced Life?

It is possible, and also really important to both you and your students. Determine your availability and clearly communicate that to the students. It may take a semester or two of teaching online to find the right pattern that you'd like to stick with. My first semester teaching online, I was available too much. I quickly learned that if I ever answered a question after 11:00 p.m., I would be expected always to answer questions that late. Learners will likely need more than what you would spend in class with them, as they may not be available at the same time you are. So logging in Monday, Wednesday, and Friday from 9:00 to 10:00 a.m. is not responsive enough to learner needs. Determining the best availability frequency is a matter of considering how your course assignment due dates are structured, your learners' needs, and your own schedule. After experimenting for several semesters, I developed a system that worked for my course, my students, and my life. At 9:00 each morning I answered any questions that had been posted overnight. At 4:00 in the afternoon I answered any questions that had been posted since 9:00 that morning. One summer, the class members and I decided we wanted the weekends off, so I had Wednesday and Friday due dates, which meant that the learners could either work over the weekend or take the weekend off (for Wednesday assignments), and finish up whatever was due Friday before the weekend as well.

**SOME THINGS TO CONSIDER**

- Will you have Sunday midnight due dates? If so, then your being unavailable to answer questions on the weekend is not fair to your learners.

- Do most of your learners work during the day? If so, then some evening availability times would be helpful.

- When are your assignments due? Learners will likely need some assistance in the hours before items are due.

- Frequency is important. Planning to spend all afternoon each Thursday to answer all questions they have for the week is not meeting learner needs.

- If you are available 24/7, this will become burdensome very quickly.

- Committing set times that learners can depend on will help set clear expectations with them so that they are not panicking that they cannot get in touch with you.

In the next lesson, Content Map, we will begin creating products for the course you've selected!

**FACULTY EXAMPLES OF BEGIN HERE**

- Share characteristics of successful learners from previous terms. For example:

  - Frequency of login

  - Time spent online

  - Time spent studying

  - Participation in office hours or study groups

- Provide recommendations from former students about how to be successful in the course. Some formats used include:

  - A letter to future students

  - Audio or video interviews with former students

  - Chat session for current students to ask questions of former students

- Have only the Begin Here section of the course visible before the term begins and for the first few days of class to ensure that students become familiar with this section.

- Include an audio or video introduction.

Share your Begin Here ideas and view others in the *Conquering the Content* Community: http://ConqueringtheContent.com/BH/Share

**2**

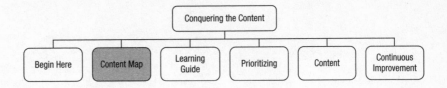
# CONTENT MAP

PLAY AUDIO INTRODUCTION

HTTP://CONQUERINGTHECONTENT.COM/CM/INTRO

**Lesson Relevance:** A Content Map is a visual representation of the topics in your course. At a glance, this image will show the organization of your content and the placement of the current topic within the context of the entire course. The Content Map will also aid learners in tagging and retrieving information for your course. Novices have a difficult time understanding the structure of a body of knowledge; the Content Map will provide that structure for learners. Creating the Content Map as the initial feature of your course development process will ensure that other items you create reflect the true scaffolding of the course content.

---

**CONQUERING THE CONTENT: A BLUEPRINT FOR ONLINE COURSE DESIGN AND DEVELOPMENT**

Lesson 2, Content Map

---

**LEARNING GOALS/OUTCOMES**

Content Map

Upon completion of this lesson, you will be able to:

- Recognize the need for presenting a content overview to learners.
- Differentiate between novices and experts.
- Categorize course topics to develop a Content Map.
- Decide on the most suitable format for a Content Map.
- Revise the Content Map as needed.
- Create appropriate files and folders needed for course development.
- Create a naming scheme for files and folders.

## LEARNING RESOURCES

Reference
- Nilson, L. B. *The Graphical Syllabus and the Outcomes Map: Communicating Your Course.* San Francisco: Jossey-Bass, 2007.

## CONTENT

Required Resource
- Smith, R. "Lesson 2, Content Map." *Conquering the Content: A Blueprint for Online Course Design and Development.* San Francisco: Jossey-Bass, 2014.

## LEARNING ACTIVITIES

Activities for This Lesson
- Translate chapter numbers into topic names.
- Determine the five to seven highest-priority subtopics for each topic/lesson.
- Categorize the subtopic components into five to seven segments and record these.
- Select a format for use in creating a Content Map.
- Organize topics so that they reflect the course and content structure.
- Create and complete a Content Map for your course.
- Revise the Content Map as needed.
- Create folders and subfolders to reflect the topic and subtopic structure.
- Name folders and subfolders according to topics/lessons.

## SELF-ASSESSMENT

Check Your Understanding
- Are you able to succinctly organize and label the topics in your course content?
- Does the structure of your course content reflect the important concepts in the course?
- Are the levels of organization reflective of the body of knowledge for your content area?
- Have you decided on a naming scheme for course files?

| "Graded" Assessments or Evidence to Proceed | • Creation of a Content Map that accurately represents content-knowledge scaffolding for your course |
| --- | --- |
| | • Creation of files and folders |
| | • Development of a naming scheme for files |

# CONTENT MAP OVERVIEW

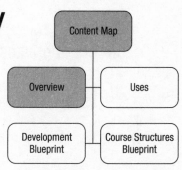

A Content Map is a visual representation of the main topics covered in your course and provides learners with the big picture, organization, and context for the topics covered in your course. This Content Map anchors the structure of knowledge scaffolding in your course. It serves as a visual guide for learners that signals how the current concepts relate to other concepts you are covering. Use of a Content Map also facilitates information retrieval.

## Chapter Conversion and Course Outline

We are going to begin by converting chapter numbers to topic names, which will allow us to create a further detailed outline for your course. With this detailed outline completed, next I will show you how the action of developing a Content Map can help you refine your ideas and accurately plan the structure of the course. Once we solidify the topics for your course, we can be confident that the remaining divisions developed for the course will accurately reflect the content and also the course structure.

Your next Action Item is to translate chapter numbers into topic names that you can use as anchoring points for the content in your course. You might also think of these topics as lessons. If you are accustomed to using chapter numbers as references to your content, this is one of those time-saving adjustments we're going to make so that your online content does not need to be updated whenever the book changes. It is a change that will benefit both you and your learners.

Translate chapter numbers into topic names using Form 6.

## CHAPTER CONVERSION

FORM 6

| CHAPTER NUMBER | TOPIC NAME |
|---|---|
| 1 | |
| 2 | |
| 3 | |
| 4 | |
| 5 | |
| 6 | |
| 7 | |
| 8 | |
| 9 | |
| 10 | |
| 11 | |
| 12 | |
| 13 | |
| 14 | |
| 15 | |
| 16 | |

Form available at www.josseybass.com/go/conqueringthecontent

Don't stress if you are not completely settled on the topic names or sequence. You will have an opportunity to review those as you are completing the Content Map. Just getting a draft will help you begin to solidify your thinking. The following figure is a preliminary outline of the Begin Here lesson of *Conquering the Content* to serve as an example. As you can see, it is OK to have some blanks at this stage of development.

| Topics with Subtopics and Sub-subtopics | | |
| --- | --- | --- |
| **Topic** | **Subtopic** | **Sub-subtopics** |
| 1 Begin Here | Good Teaching | |
| | Think Learning, Not Teaching | |
| | Advantages to Having a Course Online | |
| | Environment | Altered Learning Environment |
| | | Can Your Course Pass the Two-Minute Test? |
| | Uncomfortable OK | |
| | Online Different from Face-to-Face | |

Each topic will have a selected number of subtopics, and each subtopic will have a selected number of sub-subtopics (or concepts). I recommend clumping the sub-subtopics into no more than five to seven per subtopic. I go into the reasoning for this in Lesson 5, Content, but basically it is so that learners can group the knowledge into manageable categories and more easily retrieve that information.

**ACTION ITEM 7**

Record the five to seven highest-priority subtopics for each lesson. Repeat this step for each of the topics in your course.

Select five to seven sub-subtopics within which to organize the content for each subtopic and record these. Repeat this step for each of the subtopics in your course.

## COURSE OUTLINE

| TOPIC | SUBTOPIC | SUB-SUBTOPICS |
| --- | --- | --- |
| | | |
| | | |
| | | |
| | | |
| | | |
| | | |
| | | |
| | | |
| | | |
| | | |
| | | |
| | | |
| | | |
| | | |
| | | |
| | | |
| | | |

Form available at www.josseybass.com/go/conqueringthecontent

Once you have captured a good draft of the topics you will be using, it is time to move to the Content Map, which will function as a graphical interface for this information.

# USES OF CONTENT MAPS

In this section, we will cover the reasons for using Content Maps, how to customize them, and their recommended placement.

## Reasons to Use a Content Map

There are numerous reasons to use a Content Map in your teaching. We will focus on four: reducing the gap between novices and experts, providing information retrieval cues to your learners, providing context and location within the content, and presenting a visual element that can be processed faster than text.

### Novices vs. Experts

One of the main differences between novices and experts is that experts understand the filing system or organization of the knowledge. However, experts are so fully immersed in the content that they may not be cognizant of the schemata and structures for organizing their knowledge. As teachers, we are adept at assisting learners in understanding these structures. One of the most helpful things we can do is to explain the organization of the content in our course. Sometimes we just go with the system or organization that is in the book we are using rather than realizing that we actually use a different organizational scheme in our personal mental model. Capturing and sharing our own expert organizational structure can benefit learners.

### Information Retrieval

The Content Map signals learners regarding the topic areas that are being covered. Being exposed to this organizational structure will help learners make sense of the concepts and ideas that you will be sharing with them. In addition, they will find it much easier to retrieve information as they learn where to "file away" new concepts in relationship to their current knowledge. New concepts are sort of like the papers on my desk. If I create file folders in advance for my committees and projects for that semester or year, I will make sure that the papers get placed into those folders. If I wait until halfway into the semester to create those folders, the papers will already be piled up. I will be less likely to file things in the appropriate folder and thus more likely to be unable to retrieve them quickly. This concept is one reason that storing files electronically makes information retrieval easier: files need to be placed into a folder while being saved. (Though perhaps there may be some people reading this who have not yet discovered the great value of keeping many folders and subfolders on their computer. If you are one of these individuals, please contact me; I can help improve your life immediately!)

## Context and Location Cues

Seeing a particular topic in the context of other topics helps learners understand how this information is related to the entire course. Sometimes novices have a difficult time understanding the difference between major topics and smaller elements of the content. The Content Map helps make this distinction clear.

It is important that we keep the focus on the concepts and make it very clear to learners as to which portions of the information we are giving them are concepts and which are there for context. Because learners are unfamiliar with all of the information, it is easy for them to get hung up on support information and miss an idea that has major significance. This is one reason that parenthetical comments can be a danger. Although sidelights keep the course interesting and keep you from being bored, unless we give learners an outline or a visual of the essential concepts, they cannot be certain when we are presenting a sidelight and when we are addressing crucial information. "A good teacher," notes Steen (2007, p. 135), "can help learners by refraining from pointless digressions; such digressions may be interesting, but they also fill up short-term memory with unrelated facts. Information loss seems to occur when new data actually interferes with data that is already in working memory." In other words, tangential information may interrupt coding of the working memory. It is better to give the entire overview, drill down into some details, and then refer back to the overall structure of the information prior to drilling down into the next set of details.

## Benefits of Graphic Presentation

A visual is particularly beneficial to learners who are novices in the content area. A quick glance at the Content Map reminds learners of the current topic and the context of that topic within the entire course. For example, at the beginning of this lesson, you see that "Content Map" is the second of six lessons in this book. I am providing cues to help anchor your current location and to aid in information retrieval.

It is helpful to add appropriate images to assist learners with absorbing and processing the content. As we will see in "Instructional Design Considerations" in Lesson 5, words and pictures are processed in different ways by the brain, and engaging both processes makes it more likely that the material will be remembered (Steen, 2007).

# How to Customize the Content Map

One way I use a Content Map is at the beginning of the semester to introduce an overview of the topics we will study. Learners often have difficulty connecting the dots that exist within the subject matter. The Content Map aids this process both up front and throughout the semester by providing context and information retrieval cues.

This graphical interface represents all topics and shows the relationship between major topics and smaller subtopics. The representation here is for *Conquering the Content.*

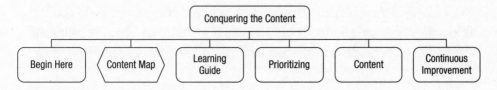

As you can see, I use a different shape to indicate the current topic for readers. For my classes, I use slide presentation or word processing software to create the Content Map, changing the color of the current topic. Highlighting a particular topic by using a distinctive shape serves the same purpose in this black-and-white environment. You may want to use shape distinctions to allow for black-and-white printing of your course content.

Shading is another way to signify the current topic.

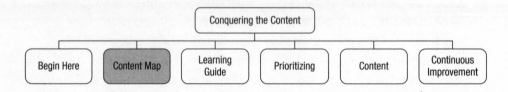

Bold outlines and text are another option. You may think of additional variations. Just be certain that whatever you select works well in both color and black and white, as learners may print in black and white.

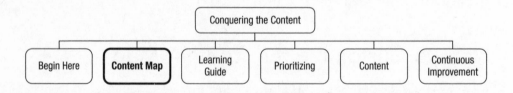

## Where to Place the Content Map

Just as I have done for each of the lessons in *Conquering the Content*, one of the first items I include in each of my online lessons is a customized form of the Content Map for that particular lesson. You will want to present this Content Map at the beginning of the course and again at each topic change. The recurring presentation will aid the learners with cues for information storage and retrieval. Repeated, consistent use of this graphic throughout the course will enable learners to become very familiar with its structure and thus very familiar with the scaffolding of knowledge in your course.

You will weave the Content Map throughout the course in increasing detail as the course progresses. For example, in the course overview, this is the Content Map I use.

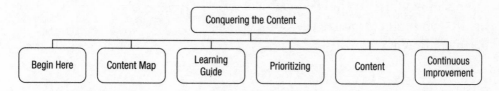

Within the lesson, I use this more detailed but narrower version of the course Content Map.

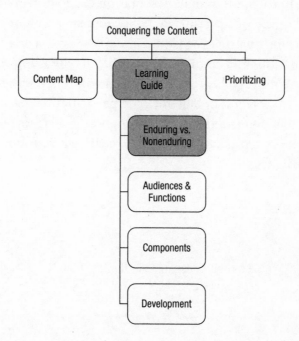

In addition, I place the specific Content Map for each individual lesson at the top of the Learning Guide for that lesson so that learners can see at a glance where this lesson fits into the context or scaffolding of their course.

# CONTENT MAP DEVELOPMENT BLUEPRINT

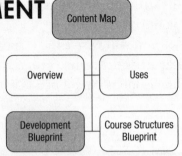

The blueprint for developing a Content Map will provide guidance for creating a final product but will also allow enough flexibility that you can customize the Content Map to fit your own needs.

## Creating a Content Map

Now that you've developed the course topic outline (Form 7/8), we are ready to move to the more visual presentation of topics using the Content Map. This will quickly communicate the overall structure of your course.

An easy way to construct the Content Map is to use a word processing or slide presentation built-in organizational chart. By using whichever software you are most comfortable with, you will find it easier to customize and update your Content Map for each particular course and/or course modification. It is important to have the highest-level (most general) Content Map fit onto one page. More detailed versions may follow in order to include all the topics.

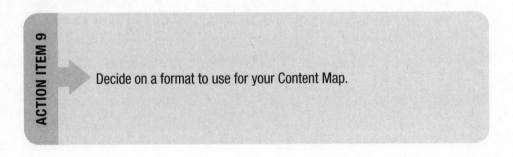

ACTION ITEM 9

Decide on a format to use for your Content Map.

## Examples

On the next pages, I provide several examples of Content Maps from colleagues who have implemented this in their courses and have received positive feedback from their learners.

Here is an example of a Content Map for Mayer's *Multimedia Learning* (2009).

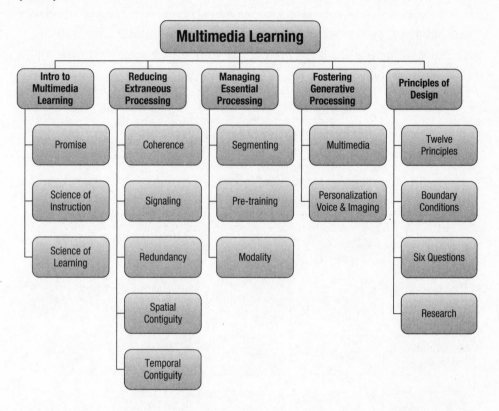

The figure on page 42 illustrates a more detailed level of that same course.

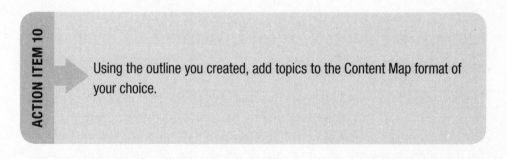

The figure on page 42 illustrates a more detailed level of that same course.

ACTION ITEM 10

Using the outline you created, add topics to the Content Map format of your choice.

An added benefit to mapping out your topics is that you can see at a glance how your course is organized and whether you are overemphasizing certain parts of the course or underemphasizing important topics.

As a rule of thumb, it is helpful to label the course topics into three to seven subtopic areas to facilitate recall. I'm not encouraging you to remove any subtopics if that particular topic has more than seven, but just to relabel them into fewer categories to aid recall. Having additional sub-subtopics within the subtopics also helps ensure that everything is covered without overwhelming the learners.

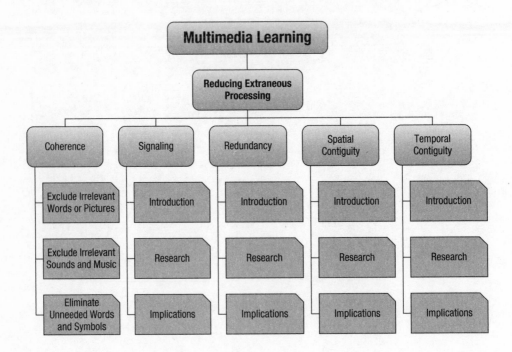

# Example of the Content Map Development Process

The next few images will provide an example of the process of developing the Content Map and using it to ensure accuracy of content presentation. These are images of actual working documents that two colleagues and I used while we were developing a grant proposal for them in radiography, so you will notice the inherit messiness of a work in progress. I think it's helpful to see a real-life example.

## Initial Outline

| Lesson | Topic | Major Points |
|---|---|---|
| 1 Review of Basic Physics | 1 Matter | 1 occupies space, inertia |
| | | 2 volume, density |
| | | 3 substance, element |
| | | 4 atomic structure |
| | | 5 electrical charge |
| | | 6 |
| | | 7 |
| | 2 Energy (E) | 1 ability to do work |
| | | 2 kinetic vs. potential |
| | | 3 types of E |
| | | |
| | | |
| | | |
| | | |
| | 3 Electromagnetic E (EME) | 1 wave/particle duality |
| | | 2 electrostatic/dynamic |
| | | 3 components of electric circuitry |
| | | 4 transformers |
| | | |
| | | |
| | | |
| 2 Characteristics of X-rays | 1 Ionizing Electromagnetic Energy | 1 travel at speed of light |
| | | 2 diverging straight lines |
| | | 3 cannot be focused |
| | | 4 absorption & scatter |
| | | 5 image receptors |
| | | 6 select max E with kVp |
| | | 7 select number of photons with mAs |

## Initial Content Map

I created this Content Map (see page 44) on the basis of the curriculum in a workbook they developed, and presented it to my colleagues. This helped them visualize how their content was being presented.

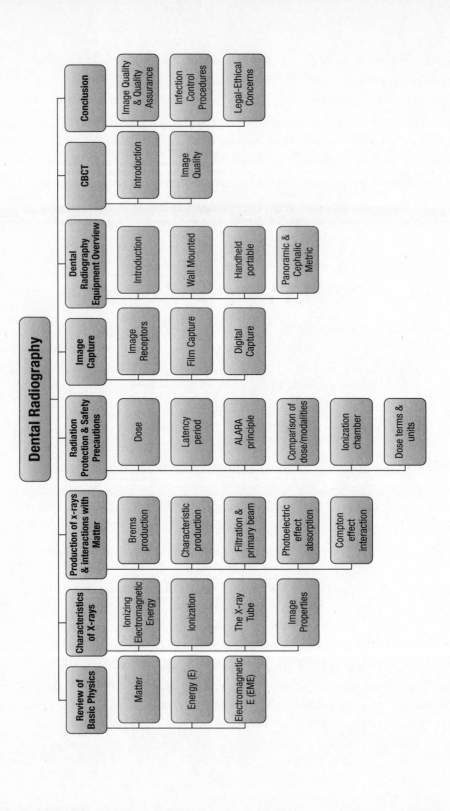

Together, we reworked the Content Map and the way we had planned the course to more accurately reflect the structure of concepts in the content. In the next image (page 46), you can see our actual working notes.

As you can see, the first draft is often not the most accurate. This exercise is very helpful to ensure that the main topics in your course are represented as such in your course structure. Working out the Content Map as the initial element of your course will ensure that the other items you develop as you go through *Conquering the Content* are accurate and will not have to be reformatted, as perhaps might be the case if you created the Content Map later in the development process.

## Choosing the Most Important Topics

Let's say that your learners are going to remember only five to nine major concepts from one lecture. What concepts would you want those to be? You would have to choose them very wisely, perhaps remembering this point: "It is better to understand new material than simply to memorize it by rote. If new material is well understood, then a few forgotten details can be derived from the context of what has been remembered. In contrast, if rote-memorized material is forgotten, it is gone" (Steen, 2007, p. 135).

Let's say that you've chosen those concepts. You'll begin by focusing on one of them. This is a segment of learning, and within this learning segment, you can also get across five to nine points. We will call each of these items a chunk. Which five to nine chunks would you like for learners to remember? Would it be better to present a hundred things and take potluck on what the novice learners remember? Or would it be better for you, the subject matter expert, to select the most important chunks so that learners completely understand those points, you have a record of what learners who leave your course know, and you can build on those concepts?

If you operate under the assumption that the learners are remembering every word you say (in reality, they never do), then you will continue to fight against reality for the remainder of the semester. If you align yourself with reality from the beginning and even relax into it, then the remainder of the semester will be much easier.

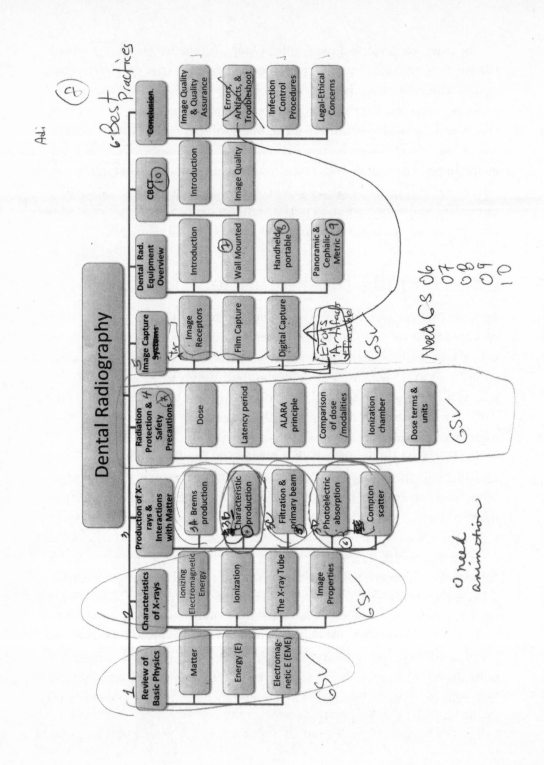

# Dental Radiography

Adi

⑧

**1 Review of Basic Physics**
- Matter
- Energy (E)
- Electromagnetic E (EME)

GSV

**2 Characteristics of X-rays**
- Ionizing Electromagnetic Energy
- Ionization
- The X-ray Tube
- Image Properties

GSV

**3 Production of X-rays & Interactions with Matter** ⑦
- 3A Brems production
- 3b Characteristic production ⑤
- 3c Filtration & primary beam ⑥
- 3d Photoelectric absorption
- 3e Compton scatter ⑥

Oral animation

**4 Radiation Protection & Safety Precautions** ⑦
- Dose
- Latency period
- ALARA principle
- Comparison of dose /modalities
- Ionization chamber
- Dose terms & units

GSV

**5 Image Capture Systems** tx
- Image Receptors
- Film Capture
- Digital Capture

Errors Artifacts Trouble

GSV

**Dental Rad. Equipment Overview**
- Introduction
- Wall Mounted ⑦
- Handheld portable ⑧
- Panoramic & Cephalic Metric ⑨

NeeA CS 06
07
08
09
10

**CBCT ⑩**
- Introduction
- Image Quality

**6-Best Practices**

**Conclusion.**
- Image Quality & Quality Assurance
- Errors, Artifacts, & Troubleshoot
- Infection Control Procedures
- Legal-Ethical Concerns

If the reality is that learners will remember only about five concepts I present, then as the subject matter expert, I want to determine those five concepts. Then we can move to the next topic or subtopic and select the next five important concepts.

What you choose to believe does not alter the truth. The truth is that learners will not remember all of the content. Other truths are that your course usually is not the only one the learners are taking and that school is most likely not the only important part of their life. I know this seems limiting, and you might be thinking, "There is no way that I can cut back on my material that much."

Think about this, though. If you cover the maximum that, according to research, a learner can absorb at one time, that is nine items. If you cover seven concepts in one module and present five to nine ideas about each of those concepts, your learners will actually understand each one. This means that they have just learned up to sixty-three ideas in one lesson. I think that is great! And what we are going to do is focus on those most meaningful portions of the course and develop learning around those chunks.

You are the expert, and you know what is essential and what is not. It is critical that you be the one selecting which information is presented. Knowing that learners' working memory is filled very quickly, we need some cues to let them know which ideas need to be captured in their working memory and which do not. We can do this by highlighting words, bolding text, outlining topics, and providing a visual cue at each essential element.

In completing the topic outline and other forms in *Conquering the Content*, the question arises: How inclusive should a lesson be? It is most manageable if it is substantial enough that you'd like to have an assignment on the lesson or topic. For example, in an English course, the instructor may have the learners write ten short papers throughout the semester, so he or she might choose to organize the course based on those ten papers. A history instructor might have twenty assignments throughout the semester and design the lesson based on those assignments. Or use the Learning Guide (as modeled at the beginning of each lesson of *Conquering the Content*) as your guide. If the learning segment is not substantial enough to warrant the information found on a Learning Guide (described in the next lesson), then perhaps that segment would benefit from being combined with another segment.

It is time to make final decisions about the topic titles and their sequence. You may normally cover ten to twenty-five or more major segments or sections in your course. We will designate each of these as a topic and hereafter use that name.

# COURSE STRUCTURES BLUEPRINT

Using some specific structural elements will keep you on track as you progress through your online course development.

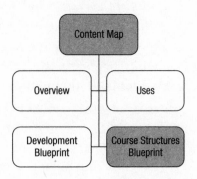

## Topics

Once you have your topics established, you can now move to create a file structure to organize and efficiently retrieve all documents associated with your online course. Creating a file and folder system in advance will keep you very organized during the remainder of the course development process. If you don't already have an efficient system of your own that you prefer to use, you might be interested in the system of files and folders I present here. I've had a few people tell me that using this file folder structure and naming scheme was the most helpful thing they've done for themselves. It is amazing how a little organization can simplify tasks.

# File Systems

Establishing a file system for your course is a good idea. And because the next lesson is about developing Learning Guides, it is beneficial to establish that structure before creating the files. The following method has proven helpful in facilitating long-term storage and retrieval of files.

# Naming Schemes

Because the topics you teach typically don't change even if the chapter numbers with a new book do, it is helpful to use a combination of topic names and lesson numbers to identify your content. Learners won't know whether red blood cells should be first or fourth, but you probably will. So "Lesson01, Red Blood Cells" is informative enough for everyone to understand what this lesson covers and its place in the learning sequence. This labeling becomes critical because it will affect everything about your lessons—for example:

- Folders
- Files
- Quiz question names
- Content file names
- Discussion topic names
- Discussion question names
- Assignment titles
- Quiz titles
- Small-group discussion titles
- Presentation files
- Audio files

The list of files you will need to name will be quite long, so using a consistent naming scheme is essential.

 **TIME-SAVING TIP**

Create a naming scheme for topics and lessons that you will use for all files you create. "Lesson01, Topic Name" is one that many people have found effective, or you can develop one that works for you.

# Folder and File Structures

The logical organization of files will make it easy to update your online courses. There may be some specific requirements for naming or organizing courses at your institution. But in the absence of those, here is a system that I, and others, have found useful.

Make a folder for each topic/lesson, using leading zeros to number the lessons below the number 10 (otherwise they won't sort correctly alphanumerically): Lesson01, Lesson02, and so on.

At some point you may need to make a subfolder for each of the components of the Learning Guide for which you have multiple files. Label these subfolders with the topic name plus the lesson number. For example, a content subfolder for Lesson01 becomes ContentL01, and a subfolder for learning resources for Lesson01 becomes LearningResourcesL01. Therefore the path for content is Lesson01/ContentL01, and for learning resources it's Lesson01/Learning ResourcesL01. You'll also want to be consistent with a naming scheme for files; for example, LGL01 refers to Learning Guide Lesson 01.

## Managing Course Structure

You will create a system of folders both in your online course and your own storage area that match up and reflect the course structure. This generic system will work regardless of the course being taught or the person working with the course. It will make just as much sense to a production assistant as it does to you. If someone offers you production assistance, you want to be able to accept at a moment's notice!

The idea of keeping the same folder and file structure both in your learning management system (LMS) or online course and your own storage area is that you will always edit outside the LMS or online course. Keep a clean copy of your LMS or online course files in your own storage area, so that you will edit in an environment with which you are familiar (word processing software or any HTML editor you may be using) and then convert to HTML (if necessary) and upload the materials to your LMS.

Whenever you need to make changes, go back to the files on your own storage device, edit again, save again using the same name as before, and re-upload, rewriting over the existing file in your LMS. All links then still remain in place.

**ACTION ITEM 12**

Make a folder for one lesson in your own storage area or on your storage device (not in the LMS).

**ACTION ITEM 13**

Make a subfolder within the folder you made in Action Item 12 for each component of the Learning Guide for which you will have multiple files—for example:

ContentL01

LearningResourcesL01

AssignmentsL01

Again, label each of these subfolders so you will know it belongs to Lesson01. Place all folders and subfolders in your own storage area.

Here is a sample for you to follow:

**File and Folder Structure**

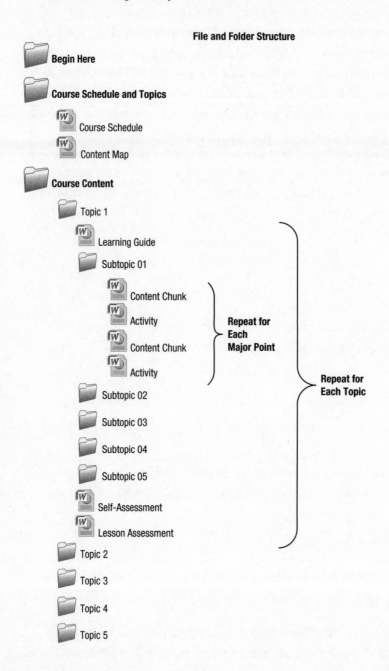

Copy the folder and subfolder structure you just created, and paste it into the main course folder enough times to have a set of folders and subfolders for each of your lessons.

Rename the new folders according to the lesson number. Use leading zeroes and number the folders for lessons below the number 10 (for example, Lesson01, Lesson02). These will be the names you see in the filing system, but in the areas where learners are able to view the names (this will be inside the LMS), it is more helpful to use topic names.

Now that the course organization is in place, you are ready to begin "filling in the blanks" for the structures you have just developed. You are well on your way to a great online course!

**CONQUERING THE CONTENT IN ACTION**

## FACULTY USES OF CONTENT MAPS

- After introducing the Content Map, an anatomy professor received positive feedback from learners indicating that they were able to better organize the course content in their minds with use of the Content Map.

- The same faculty member decided to create a large poster-size Content Map to display in the laboratory (for a blended course).

- A humanities professor provides a second copy of the Content Map with the current lesson unlabeled so that learners have a practice opportunity.

- A history professor created an online drag-and-drop activity to help learners become familiar with the Content Map and thus the structure of the course content.

# 3

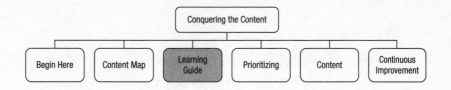

Conquering the Content

| Begin Here | Content Map | Learning Guide | Prioritizing | Content | Continuous Improvement |

# LEARNING GUIDE

 PLAY AUDIO INTRODUCTION ▶ HTTP://CONQUERINGTHECONTENT.COM/LG/INTRO

**Lesson Relevance:** Once you have established the Content Map, the next step is to develop Learning Guides. The Learning Guide serves as a course development map and will enable you to separate enduring content from the logistics of the course; this is the key to facilitating updates for your course. The Learning Guide is also beneficial to learners by providing a one-page overview of the lesson and delineating a clear pathway of progression through the course. This structural feature will be the framework for each of the lessons in your course. I suggest that you create one Learning Guide for each topic in the course and do so before developing any portion of the course itself.

### CONQUERING THE CONTENT: A BLUEPRINT FOR ONLINE COURSE DESIGN AND DEVELOPMENT

Lesson 3, Learning Guide

### LEARNING OBJECTIVES

Learning Guide

Upon completion of this lesson, you will be able to:

- Recall two audiences for Learning Guides.
- Recall the purposes of Learning Guides.
- Recognize the components of Learning Guides.
- Customize for your own use the Learning Guide Blueprint.
- Create one Learning Guide file for each topic/lesson using the Content Map developed in Lesson 2.
- Document objectives, resources, learning activities, self-assessments, learning assessments, and points possible for each lesson.

## LEARNING RESOURCES

References

- Content Map you developed in Lesson 2.
- Naming scheme you developed in Lesson 2.
- American Association of Higher Education Assessment Forum. *Nine Principles of Good Practice for Assessing Student Learning,* 1996. http://www.academicprograms.calpoly.edu/pdfs/assess/nine_principles_good_practice.pdf
- Comeaux, P. *Assessing Online Learning.* San Francisco: Jossey-Bass, 2005.
- Finkelstein, J. *Learning in Real Time: Synchronous Teaching and Learning Online.* San Francisco: Jossey-Bass, 2006.
- Walvoord, B. E., and Anderson, V. A. *Effective Grading: A Tool for Learning and Assessment.* San Francisco: Jossey-Bass, 1998.

## CONTENT

Required Resource

- Smith, R. "Lesson 3, Learning Guide." *Conquering the Content: A Blueprint for Online Course Design and Development.* San Francisco: Jossey-Bass, 2014.

## LEARNING ACTIVITIES

Activities for This Lesson

- Download Learning Guide Blueprint from http://Conqueringthe Content.com
- Customize the Learning Guide Blueprint or develop a format of your own to create Learning Guides.
- Using the Content Map developed in Lesson 2, create one Learning Guide file for each topic.
- Save these files with your chosen file-naming scheme.
- Determine dates for lessons and record these.
- Record the course title and lesson topic on each Learning Guide.
- Create a small image of the Content Map for inclusion in the Learning Guide.
- Document objectives or learning outcomes for each lesson.
- Identify references and resources for lessons.
- Distinguish between required and supplemental resources.
- Locate links to resources used in each Learning Guide.
- Identify and develop learning activities for each learning objective.
- Develop detailed directions for each assignment.
- Document required resources, content, learning activities, self-assessments, lesson assessments, and points possible for each lesson.
- Create self-assessments for each lesson.
- Plan and create assessments for each lesson.

## SELF-ASSESSMENT

Check Your Understanding

- Have you selected a blueprint to use for Learning Guides?
- Are you able to create a workable Learning Guide?

## LESSON ASSESSMENT

"Graded" Assessments or Evidence to Proceed

- Creation of Learning Guides that will be used to guide the development of your online course and be presented to learners in each lesson of your online course.

# ENDURING VS. NONENDURING CONTENT

You are investing a substantial amount of time in developing your online course. It is to your distinct advantage to ensure that you will be able to reuse portions of your course from term to term. Therefore, it is essential that you separate the enduring elements of your course from the nonenduring elements, lest the logistics cause you to have to redo materials each time. Enduring elements include topics, concepts and perhaps assignments, projects, and learning activities if you reuse these for more than one term. Nonenduring elements include logistics: chapter numbers, page references, dates, and times. This separation will be a huge time saver because it will free you from updating portions of your course when the book changes, when you offer the course in a different length (15 weeks, 10 weeks, 8 weeks, 5 weeks), or when new content is available in your area of expertise. If you develop an online course and miss the opportunity to separate logistics from enduring content, you are creating more work for yourself instead of less. Learning Guides are the key to this separation. If you adopt only one item from *Conquering the Content*, I recommend the Learning Guide, as it will have the largest impact on your time and also on the organization of your course (and hence your learners' perception of the course).

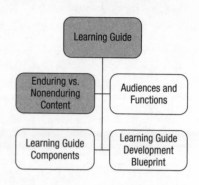

>  **TIME-SAVING TIP**
>
> Separate all logistical elements of the course from the enduring content. Dates and chapter and page numbers change. Chapter and page numbers should be referenced in the Learning Guides, *never* within the enduring content of your course. Dates also need to be separated from the enduring content. Dates may be listed in the Learning Guides as well. In addition, a separate table of dates and topics covered along with assignment due dates will prove helpful to learners.

Originally trained as a research scientist, I typically do not use the words "always" and "never." I am using them here very purposefully, so please take note; this is an important time-saving tip for you!

One of the crucial principles for keeping your course easy to update is *never* to embed book page numbers or chapter references within course content, quizzes, assignments, discussions, feedback, or any other portion of the course. Book page numbers and chapter references should appear only in the Learning Guides. The reason is that when the book is revised, you will know exactly where to go in order to update the chapter and page references if the Learning Guide and Course Schedule are the only places you have those references. Otherwise you might have to search through hundreds (or thousands) of pages of content, quiz questions, or question feedback for chapter and page references in order to update those.

| NONENDURING |
| --- |
| Dates |
| Chapter number references |
| Page numbers |
| Assignment due dates |
| Quiz dates (day of week) |
| Schedule/sequence of topics |
| Announcements |

| ENDURING |
| --- |
| Objectives |
| Concepts |
| Topic names |
| Assignment content (possibly) |
| Quiz questions |
| Projects (possibly) |
| Discussion topics/questions (possibly) |

ACTION ITEM 16

Download the Learning Guide Blueprint from http://Conqueringthe
Content.com

ACTION ITEM 17

Customize the Learning Guide Blueprint or develop a format of your own
to use.

ACTION ITEM 18

Using the Content Map and file-naming scheme you developed in
Lesson 2, create one Learning Guide file for each topic.

ACTION ITEM 19

Save each of these files with the file-naming scheme you developed in
Lesson 2 (perhaps LG01TopicName, LG02TopicName, and so on).

# AUDIENCES AND FUNCTIONS

There are two main audiences for Learning Guides. Both you (the faculty member developing the course) and the learners will benefit from using them. I use the exact same version of the Learning Guide both for my own course development needs and for learner use. There is a big payoff from creating these Learning Guides. The following chart highlights the functions of the Learning Guide for faculty and for learners.

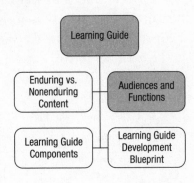

| LEARNING GUIDE AUDIENCES AND FUNCTIONS | |
|---|---|
| **Audience** | **Function** |
| Faculty | • Assists in planning the course |
| | • Provides architectural structure for the course |
| | • Facilitates communication of course requirements to learners |
| | • Anchors logistical information about the lesson |
| | • Serves as a course development map |
| | • Prioritizes course development |
| Learners | • Anchors the learning experience |
| | • Serves as a checklist for learning |
| | • Communicates clear expectations |
| | • Consolidates scope of lesson in one document |
| | • Signals timely progression pathway through the course |

# Faculty

Learning Guides serve multiple functions in the course development process for you as a faculty member. Remember, the same version that works for learners will also work for you, so this is a valuable investment of time.

## Assists in Planning the Course

It is important to take a holistic look at the course, stepping back from the fall semester/spring semester/summer term way of thinking. This can be a difficult step for faculty. Many of us think in terms of weeks of the semester or "from now until spring break, I normally do this." I even had an instructor tell me once that she could not teach a class on Tuesdays and Thursdays because she'd always taught it on Mondays, Wednesdays, and Fridays; all her lectures and assignments were divided up that way, and it would be too hard to alter it all. We sometimes lock ourselves into a routine and forget to take a look at the knowledge as a whole rather than in terms of its division into class meetings. Instead, overall course structure should be independent of time and of book chapters.

>  **TIME-SAVING TIP**
>
> Overall course structure should be independent of time and of book chapters.

Online courses are best designed so that they may be taught regardless of the time frame in which they are offered—not Week 1 and Week 2, for example, but Lesson 1 and Lesson 2. We need to look at the information and subject that we teach, not the time frame. In the future, who knows if we will still be offering fifteen-week semesters? What if we decide to allow learners to concentrate on one subject at a time and saturate themselves in that one course until they've completed the requirements in a reduced time frame, then move to the next course? We want to be ready for all that. Accelerated five- to eight-week courses are already being offered at my institution along with the regular semester-length courses. Competency-based courses are also becoming more popular. The course structure proposed in *Conquering the Content* will work with all of these options, ensuring that you can be flexible and that your course can easily be offered in multiple formats.

Online courses are also independent of book chapters. If we write the course according to a particular book, we'll have to revamp the entire course as soon as the book is revised. However, we tend to teach the same topics regardless of which edition of the text is used, so the topic names provide a more enduring structure.

## Provides Architectural Structure

Components of lessons are those modeled in this book:

Content Map

Audio introduction

Lesson relevance

Learning Guide

Content 1

Activity 1

Content 2

Activity 2

Content 3

Activity 3

Self-assessment

Lesson assessment

Each lesson has a Learning Guide and sets up the framework for the course and progression through the course. It also allows you to make a plan and then begin to fill in the blanks as you have time.

## Facilitates Communication of Requirements to Learners

A Learning Guide is a succinct checklist that contains everything learners need to do for one lesson. You will never add items to the course content online without updating the Learning Guide; therefore, components within the course are always reflected there, so learners will not find assignments or content unexpectedly within the course that the Learning Guide does not contain. Thus it is like a travel guide to your course.

## Anchors Logistical Information About the Lesson

The Learning Guide is where references to book pages and chapter numbers appear. In fact, this is the only place where there are references to specifics of the book. Remember that you are trying to ensure that your course is easily updatable. When book references appear only on this page in the course materials, you know exactly where to go to alter chapter and page references when a new edition of the book is adopted.

## Serves as a Course Development Map

Learning Guides will serve as the blueprint from which to develop a course; therefore, anything you need to create or place in the LMS for a lesson will be placed in the Learning Guide. Subsequently it provides a checklist to use for course development.

### Prioritizes Course Development

After you have developed Learning Guides for each lesson, you will look at the entire course and determine priorities before developing the individual components of the course. The prioritization process, which is covered in detail in Lesson 4, will be based on the amount of time you have before the course begins.

## Learners

Everything learners need to access or complete for a lesson will appear in the Learning Guide for that lesson. In other words, if it is an expectation for the learners, it needs to be in the Learning Guide.

### Anchors the Learning Experience

Adding an online component to our course (blended learning) or moving the entire course online increases the number of places where content may be found. Unless there is an anchoring point for the content, it can seem scattered among the book, face-to-face environment, journal articles, discussion threads, assignments, and other tools we use to deliver the learning experience. The Learning Guide serves as the anchor point for all resources to be accessed for one lesson.

### Serves as a Checklist for Learning

It is helpful to make the Learning Guide a printable resource that guides participants' learning both online and offline. It also serves as a checklist for learners so they will be assured that their work is complete when they finish all of the items in the Learning Guide. If you have ever received an email from a learner that indicates you should "let me know if there is anything else I need to do for my work," then you recognize the importance of providing learners with their own way to manage their tasks.

### Ensures That Learners Understand What Is Expected of Them

Because you will indicate that everything the learner needs to do is recorded in the Learning Guide and that the learner needs to do everything in the Learning Guide in order to complete this lesson, you make your expectations clear. You don't want participants "hunting around" the course to figure out what they are supposed to do. Your clear and explicit expectations will ensure that learners do not need to interrupt their learning to contact you (possibly interrupting you) and to wait for a reply.

## Consolidates Scope of Lesson in One Document

Learning Guides enable learners to plan their week and to schedule course work from your class along with that of the other courses they are taking. Providing the entire scope of the lesson in the Learning Guide and not expecting the learners to discover assignments within the online course helps both you and the course participants stay organized.

## Signals Timely Progression Pathway Through the Course

One purpose of the Learning Guide is to guide learners through the lessons in your course and provide a pathway for their progression through the course. Learning Guides serve as guideposts or stepping-stones to allow clear progression from one lesson to the next. A clear pathway through the course is essential for learner success.

# LEARNING GUIDE COMPONENTS

You likely have all the components of the Learning Guide in your course already, though they may not be consolidated into one place. Here is a list of what you need to include:

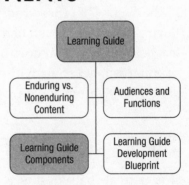

- Dates of the lesson
- Identification of the lesson
- Learning goals/outcomes
- Learning resources
  - Required resources
  - Additional resources

- Learning activities

- Self-assessment

- Lesson assessment

- Number of points earned on this lesson and total points so far in the course

I hope that by now I've convinced you of the value of Learning Guides, so let's begin!

# LEARNING GUIDE DEVELOPMENT BLUEPRINT

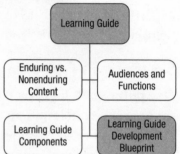

This lesson and Lesson 5, Content, are the most challenging in the book. If you do not complete the activities in this lesson, developing your course will be more difficult for you.

Planning your course through these Learning Guides is the key to good course organization, which in turn is the key to your learners' being confident of their direction in the course. It is also your ticket to a semester that is not filled with telephone calls, emails, and questions regarding processes in the course. In other words, the payoff for the exercises in this lesson is huge. The format set out here has worked for me and for many of my colleagues. If this format does not work for you, then alter it or make up one of your own, but some type of organizer like this for your learners and your own planning will prove to be very helpful.

## The Rewards of Preparation Time

It is critical that you know what is going to happen throughout your course before the semester begins. The suicide method of course development (trying to stay one to two weeks ahead of the learners) is troublesome for everyone in the course and everyone around you.

All design and development activities should be completed before the semester begins, and any preparation time you spend prior to the semester will save you time during the semester. In my experience, when I waited until during the semester to do those same tasks, it took me ten to thirty times longer than when I addressed those tasks before the semester began. The time investments in course design and development prior to the beginning of the course are wise ones. It appears to be a lot of work to develop the Learning Guides, and it is, but, as you've seen, the benefits are numerous.

 **TIME-SAVING TIP**

If you use recorded narration as an element of content in your online course, be certain that the narration is enduring. This means leaving out references to the test "next Thursday" or other upcoming or past dates.

Use "next time" or "the next segment" rather than "tomorrow" or "chapter 2." It is even better to use "in the segment on [topic name]" rather than "the next topic" because, at some point, you might reorder the sequence of lessons.

## Dates

Because learners will likely print out the Learning Guide to use while they are working offline, having the dates for this lesson readily available will help keep them on track. This will also reinforce the information you provide in the Course Schedule. If there is a particular range of dates when learners are expected to begin and end the lesson, note them near the top of the Learning Guide.

Determine the dates that each lesson will be covered and record those at the top of the Learning Guide for each lesson.

# Identification

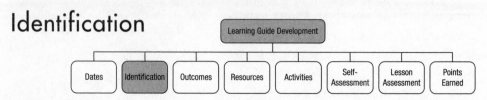

Several pieces of identification will be advantageous for learners to have on the Learning Guides.

## Course Title and Lesson Topic

Make certain that the Learning Guide is identified with the course title and the topic/lesson name. We hope that other faculty members at your institution will also adopt Learning Guides and that learners should be able to distinguish the guide for your course and this particular lesson at a glance.

## Content Map

It will also be helpful to have a small image of the Content Map with the current topic highlighted within the structure so that learners have a visual to provide the context of this topic within the entire course. As mentioned in Lesson 2, Content Map, this aids information retrieval and assists novices with understanding the filing system of the course content.

Record the course title and lesson topic on each Learning Guide.

Create a small image of the Content Map showing the particular lesson highlighted or with a different shape.

# Learning Objectives/Outcomes, or "What I Need to Know"

I find that first- and second-year undergraduate learners are more comfortable with casual titles in the Learning Guide. Use the ones I have here, or create a variation of your own that is customized for your learners. Alter the title and formatting to suit your situation.

I've found that in some cases, objectives are those things that both we and our learners avoid. They can be sort of a pain for faculty, and many times (especially if we don't customize the objectives) learners just skip right over them. However, there is a better way. Objectives form one of the fundamental elements of instruction. In a nutshell, we need to tell learners what we want them to know, provide some instruction and learning activities to help them learn it, and assess them to see whether they "got it" or whether we need additional instructional activities.

## Alignment

If you include an objective, you also need to include content, a learning activity, and an assessment for that objective. If you do not have (or do not wish to add) a learning activity and an assessment, then delete the objective, as it isn't really valid for your course.

Similarly, if you have a learning activity and an assessment with no objective, you need to make a decision about whether you want to add an objective or drop the activity and the assessment.

Basically, in order for your course to be appropriately aligned, you need to ensure there are no orphaned objectives, content, learning activities, or assessment items. All objectives should have learning activities and assessments. Now is a good time to make sure that all of these components are aligned, because they're all part of the Learning Guide. I've included a table here that you can use to help ensure alignment of your course.

| OBJECTIVE | CONTENT | LEARNING ACTIVITY | ASSESSMENT |
|---|---|---|---|
| | | | |
| | | | |
| | | | |
| | | | |
| | | | |
| | | | |
| | | | |
| | | | |
| | | | |
| | | | |
| | | | |
| | | | |

Form available at www.josseybass.com/go/conqueringthecontent

## Components of Quality Objectives

Knowing that you need an objective and writing good ones are two different things, so let's talk more about recommendations for objectives. An acronym frequently used to prompt us to remember the components of objectives is SMART. Objectives should be

Specific: What exactly will be done?

Measurable: Can you gather data to show these results?

Attainable: Is it possible to achieve the objective with the instructional methods and scope of the course?

Relevant: Does this relate to the goals of the overall program or degree?

Time-bound: When does it need to be accomplished?

We are trying to spur our learners to action, so we should write objectives such that they can take action after reading them. Use of verbs associated with the Revised Bloom's Taxonomy (Anderson and Krathwohl, 2001) will aid in this process.

Spend some time making the learning objectives meaningful. You can often find a version of these in your instructor's manual, but is that really what you teach? Use those published objectives as a basis to customize the learning objectives for the course you teach. Few faculty members follow an entire book; the objectives will also probably need to be altered. Some institutions have distinct preferences about using "objectives" or "learning outcomes," so use what fits your situation.

**ACTION ITEM 23**

Develop objectives or outcomes for each lesson, and record them in the appropriate Learning Guide.

Here is a way to take a fresh look at your course. If it were up to you for your favorite niece or nephew to learn the first objective, what would be the best way for her or him to learn that lesson? Are there some experiences she or he would need to have? Are there some books that would be useful? Are there some people you'd like her or him to meet?

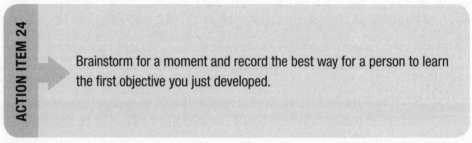

**ACTION ITEM 24**

Brainstorm for a moment and record the best way for a person to learn the first objective you just developed.

| OBJECTIVE | BEST WAY TO LEARN THIS |
| --- | --- |
| | |

**ACTION ITEM 25**

Repeat Action Item 24 for each of the objectives of the lessons of your course.

# Learning Resources, or "Tools to Help Me Learn"

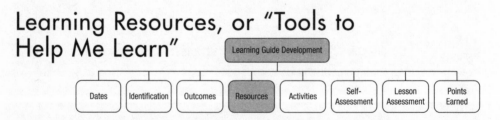

These are the references learners will need to access for this lesson. It is helpful to divide these into "required resources" and "supplemental resources" categories.

List any presentation of content here. Perhaps you have supplied recorded lectures, course notes, online text, some type of video or audio, or a slide presentation of the content in your online course. Note these in the content section, and provide the link to those resources so that learners will know where to find them. References to book pages go here. The Learning Guide and the Course Schedule (discussed in Lesson 6) are the only two places in the course to list book pages and chapter references.

Links to journal articles, websites, or other resources that learners will use for this lesson belong in this section of the Learning Guide as well. If you list a website or link, you also need to provide additional information:

- What do you want the learners to do with that link? Is that a major task or a minor one?

- Do you want them to just skim the contents or grasp the details?

- Is this an overview or a detailed version of an important concept?

Give learners the context into which this website falls and the reason they are directed to it:

- What are they supposed to do when they get there?

- What are the supposed to bring back?

- Where do they turn this in?

If you can't answer those questions, reconsider whether the link should be included.

As mentioned, distinguish between required and supplemental resources. Supplemental resources are helpful for learners who want to explore the topic further, but for those who want to complete the assignment and quickly move forward, you want to make it clear that those resources are indeed optional.

**ACTION ITEM 26**

Identify references or resources your learners will need to complete each lesson and record those in the appropriate Learning Guide.

> Distinguish between required resources and supplemental resources so that it is clear where learners need to focus their attention.

## Gathering Resources

After developing your Learning Guides, use them to gather links to your library's electronic resources. You will be able to do this efficiently because you have listed all the articles you need. My hope is that your library has subscriptions to online journals and that you have the ability to link directly from your course to the journal. If this is the case, such direct linking is typically considered the best approach. Verify links to ensure that learner access is available via the link provided.

By creating all the Learning Guides in advance, you can be very efficient about creating individual components of the Learning Guides. Let's say you need twenty quizzes, so when you have five to ten minutes between meetings or are waiting for someone, you can churn out a quiz question or two. Or maybe you want learners to do an assignment four times during the semester and want to create a form for it. If you are among the fortunate who have assistance with course development, you can be ready to take advantage of that assistance by having completed all the Learning Guides in advance. For example, you can say, "I need these twenty quizzes, and here are the questions," rather than coming to that person or emailing him or her twenty different times and saying, "Here's another quiz."

## Making Connections

You might talk with your librarian about copyright requests for these articles and to get his or her recommendation about the best way to gain access to the articles for your learners. Some facilities have access to a Citrix server, where articles and images sensitive to copyright may be stored so that learners can have access without compromising the integrity of the materials. Other provisions may be in place at your institution.

Every institution has different ways of working with academic computing, library staff, online learning staff, and information technology staff who are involved with these types of resources. You should get to know all of these individuals because you depend on them for your courses, and you want them to know you and know that you are cooperative and congenial. You might survive a few weeks if the boss is mad at you, but if the person who helps you get over the bumps in your online course is mad at you, life can be unbearable.

**ACTION ITEM 28**

Reserve or find links to resources that you have referenced in the "Tools to Help Me Learn" section.

# Learning Activities, or "What I Need to Do"

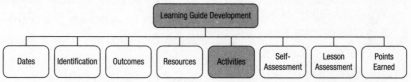

List specific assignments here. Perhaps you have discussion questions for the learners to answer or an assignment for them to complete. Remember that this is a checklist they are using to make sure they do all their work, so anything that needs to be completed should be listed.

For each assignment, learners need this information:

- What to do.

- How to do it.

- How it will be graded—that is, what is important and what is not important in grading.

- How many points it is worth.

- How these points compare to the overall number of points in the course.

- How this falls into the context of the course. Is this a large, major assignment or topic or a lesser or minor point?

- Where they turn in the assignment.

- What they should title this assignment. (Provide the file name.)

- How they should label this assignment.

- The time it is due.

- What sorts of reference materials they should use to complete this assignment.

- Whether collaboration with other learners is an option.

This looks like a daunting list, but answering these questions in advance will allow you and your learners to avoid much confusion; moreover, the learners will feel comfortable and confident that all is under control. It will also prevent you from having to answer these questions individually from the learners. Once again, this upfront investment of time will pay off well later. It is easier than you think to get all these answers into your assignments.

Here is an assignment example that answers these questions:

- Cell Organelle: Individual project using current references provided in Lesson 01.

- Describe the major function of one organelle of a eukaryotic cell in 75–100 words.

- 50 points out of 1,000 total points for the course. [Link to grading rubric.] See sample assignment.

> ### ⏲ TIME-SAVING TIP
>
> One easy way to figure grades is to have all courses total 1,000 points, with grades based on total points. It takes 900 points to get an A, 800 to get a B, and so forth. You can plan this from the beginning. If you want a certain portion to count 30 percent, make it worth 300 points. Using this method, learners will be clear about what their grades are at all times.

- Submit in the Assignments tool labeled "Assignment 01."

- Label: "LastnameFirstnameA01."

- Due October 21 at 5:00 p.m.

- External references preferred.

- Collaboration with other students encouraged.

In order for learners to understand how the assignment of points fits into the context of the entire course, it is helpful to have this worked out in advance. One easy way to figure points is to have all courses worth 1,000 points. You can plan this from the beginning. If you want the lab portion to be worth 30 percent, you can make it worth 300 points. Then you can adjust test or assignment scores accordingly. In this way, learners will be clear about what their grades are at all times. Grades can be based on total points. It takes 900 points to get an A, 800 to get a B, and so forth. I've done this for years, and it makes for fewer questions and less complication with grade calculations both for me and for the learners.

Chickering and Gamson (1987) tell us to set high expectations, and part of setting expectations is modeling examples for learners. Giving a sample completed assignment that you deem to be excellent work is sometimes an appropriate option. In creative assignments, you might want to give learners freedom to use their own imaginations and not limit their ideas to an example you provide. But on assignments for which you know what you want, it is good to show the learners what that is. The better they understand your expectations, the more likely they are to meet them.

**ACTION ITEM 29**

Identify learning activities and assignments you will have for learners for each lesson and record these in the appropriate Learning Guide.

Develop detailed directions for each assignment and learning activity so that learners know exactly where to turn in or submit evidence of their learning. Include specific identifier information (file name, subject heading, and any other information you prefer) that the learner needs in order to submit work. Determine the dates and times that assignments will be due.

## Active Learning Opportunities

It is crucial to provide learners with opportunities to reinforce the content we've presented. Kruse (2005) indicates that all stimuli to sensory storage are processed in real time, so as new information comes in, it replaces the previous information. These items will be held for only about thirty seconds unless a memory aid such as repetition or chunking is used. Research shows that the timing of these reinforcements is critical. People have difficulty remembering even three elements after eighteen seconds. Further research has shown that the duration of short-term memory may be much shorter than eighteen seconds, decaying after about two seconds (Marsh, Sebrechts, Hicks, and Landau, 1997).

There are several software options available that allow you to create multiple learning activities, offering learners an opportunity to spend more time on task, interact with the content, and reinforce the information in short-term memory. Most of these options provide an excellent return on your investment of time spent producing the activities. For a single input of information, you can generate multiple exercises for your learners. There are also options available for learners to create study aids and share them with each other. This also supports social learning.

One of Chickering and Gamson's teaching principles (1987), "Give rich and rapid feedback," tells us that we need to give both formative assessments (administered along the way; designed to assist with determining learning needs) and summative assessments (those that evaluate the student's learning). If the assessments are opportunities to learn, then we are using every opportunity to refine the learner's knowledge as well as evaluate and refine our course. One exercise may provide both assessment and evaluation information, but in general I will separate the two in this lesson.

Merrill's premise (2002) that practice which includes an opportunity to make mistakes, evaluate performance, and correct those mistakes is one of the best ways to learn also directs us toward formative assessments with opportunities for feedback and the option to improve performance.

Both Chickering and Gamson (1987) and Merrill (2002) point toward self-assessment opportunities for learners. It is important that learners have the opportunity to verify their own learning and remediate themselves prior to a graded evaluation. In addition, functional and authentic assessments are becoming much more commonplace. The American Association of Higher Education Assessment Forum (1996), for example, has established assessment principles.

An additional function of assessment and evaluation in an online course is to provide you with information about learners' understanding of the concepts. There are many ways in the face-to-face environment to see in learners' faces whether they got the point just made; blank stares, for example, are a sign that they didn't understand a word of what you just presented. As instructors, we have to find a way to communicate this same information back to online learners. It is important to build in feedback mechanisms so you have a sense of when additional explanations or the opportunity to quicken the pace of the content are needed.

## Specific Discussion Assignments

We need to distinguish between discussion questions for the discussion area and paragraph or essay-type questions on an exam. Essay or paragraph questions have one correct answer, often with multiple points to the answer. If those same questions are placed in an online course and the learners are told to "discuss," it will be very difficult to stimulate interaction. After the first person presents the correct answer and the second person rewords it to say the same or a similar thing but in different words, what will the remainder of the learners have to write? At that point, the remaining learners are limited to "I agree," "I think that is a good point," "I disagree because . . .," and other limited responses.

Good discussion questions elicit discussion. It helps if you can have learners bring in their own experience and expertise to exemplify concepts. An additional option is to assign learners a role to play in the discussion of a particular topic. Workable roles include pro and con stance, the summarizer for the group, and the questioner who asks for clarification. Another technique is to assign roles corresponding to the stakeholders in the scenario you have presented. For example, when presenting a case in which a controversial pesticide is being used, stakeholders might include the farmer, nearby homeowners, other competing farmers in the area, the seed company, the company selling the pesticide, consumers of the food being produced, grocery stores supplied by the farmer, extension personnel, and many more. In a hospital scenario, stakeholders could include physicians, nurses, the patient, family members of the patient, hospital staff, the billing office, the medical supplies department, and the pharmacy.

It is sometimes difficult to get individuals in a group each to "tell us something about yourself," but if instead you give them specifics to address—"Tell us your name, where you are from, your major, and, if you have pets, what kind"—it makes it much easier for people to talk about themselves. The same approach is effective in a discussion area when you present a question, even a controversial one, and want people to engage in discussion. It is much easier if you tell them something to talk about. For example, you might ask learners to present a lesson plan on a particular topic. The follow-up instructions might be to reply to at least one of the other learners with a positive suggestion about how to improve his or her lesson plan.

It is vital to have a deadline on first posts if a second post is expected during the week. Otherwise, learners might wait until the night of the deadline to make their first posts and then other learners cannot complete their assignment because their colleagues have procrastinated. So you might, for example, make first posts due on Wednesday at noon and follow-ups due by Friday at midnight, or create a similar schedule that fits the pace of progression in the course.

# Self-Assessment, or "How to Know If I Am Ready for Grading"

Accrediting agencies suggest giving learners an opportunity to assess their own learning progress before they are given a graded assessment. This is an opportunity for the learners to find the weak areas in their knowledge and review them prior to the graded assessment.

Self-assessments are varied in format:

- A description of knowledge: "You should be able to define all the new terms in this lesson and be able to apply those terms in appropriate situations."

- A quiz: "You should be able to score 100 percent on the practice quiz."

- Behavioral/clinical: "You should be able to take blood pressure accurately within two minutes at least three times out of four attempts."

- An activity from the book: "You should be able to complete all the review exercises at the end of the chapter."

Moreno (2004) found that explanatory feedback promotes higher scores and reduces cognitive load compared to corrective feedback. It is thus better to tell learners why an answer is correct or incorrect rather than just to say that it is right or wrong. At the moment of incorrect thinking, you can correct their thinking and explain why it is this way or that.

It is helpful to incorporate retesting and lots of practice. Self-tests, tests without scores, and scores that do not count are all beneficial. Some faculty members allow learners to have unlimited practice on quizzes and record only the highest score. Others take an average of all scores so that learners have some responsibility for good performance the first time taking the quiz. Still others record the first score as a grade, but then allow learners to continue to take the quiz as practice in preparation for later assessments. A final option is to record the last score. Your choice depends on your goal for quizzes or tests and your philosophy about their function within the entirety of your course.

In a medical terminology course I taught, I encouraged the learners to take the weekly quizzes five times (there were alternate questions on the quizzes, so learners did not get the same quiz each time), and I recorded only the highest score. I did this for two reasons. I knew that the more frequently they practiced and the more repetition they had with the terms, the better off they would be when it came to the major test. In addition, I did not want any of the learners to make a perfect grade on the first or second attempt and then be afraid of taking the quiz again for practice for fear of messing up their perfect score.

That is what I thought worked best in my situation, but other people choose other ways of managing quizzes. You have to customize your approach to fit your teaching style, learners, subject matter, and institutional environment.

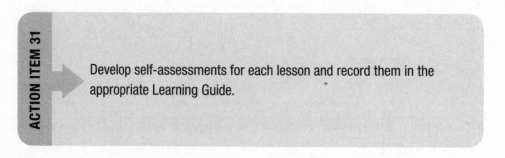

**ACTION ITEM 31**

Develop self-assessments for each lesson and record them in the appropriate Learning Guide.

# Lesson Assessment, or "How Do I Earn Points on What I Have Learned?"

Any opportunities the learners will have for gaining points from this lesson should be listed here. It might be a quiz or an assignment on this lesson, or it may be the portion of the unit test that covers the lesson. Learners need to know how and when they will be graded on this material.

## Advance Planning

Like you, your learners are extremely busy individuals and need to be able to plan their lives in advance. One way I help my learners is to commit to due dates and test dates at the beginning of the semester so they can arrange work schedules, babysitters, and other help. I do not change due dates or test dates. If the course needs adjustment, I might change the amount of material covered on the exam or assignment, but not the date. This commitment to the learners and my respect for them set a tone of professional courtesy in the course that ends up working to everyone's advantage.

## Authentic Assessments

It is increasingly important to use learner assessments that fit real-world circumstances. Especially with nontraditional-age learners who have many life experiences to share, it is a benefit to them and their fellow learners if they can incorporate their prior knowledge into their assignments.

In addition, just because someone can answer questions about how to develop a presentation doesn't mean that the person can actually develop a presentation. It is an advantage for learners to practice in situations like those in real life within a learning venue rather than waiting until they get to a job situation. Our institutions and workplaces benefit when graduates are already adept at working in teams, comfortable with producing and presenting ideas to others, and finding information and communicating it to diverse audiences.

The question to ask is, "What is it I am trying to teach the learners?" If the answer is, "How to write," then you need to see examples of their writing to know if they are able to write correctly. Answering multiple-choice questions about the correct way to write is not the same as demonstrating the ability to write. And if learners need to know how to identify appropriate settings on a machine, then they need to be shown the machine and asked to identify the appropriate settings for specific situations, not answer multiple-choice or true-false questions about the correct settings. If you don't measure performance of the task itself, you just measure learners' recognition of the terms related to the task. The two are not the same. An added benefit of authentic assessments is that they are much more interesting and motivating to the learners and build more confidence when they have performed well.

To see how important authentic assessments are, ask yourself who you would rather have cut your hair: someone who has scored 100 percent on ten fifty-question multiple-choice tests about cutting hair but has no experience, or someone who has actually cut the hair of multiple individuals but taken no written tests? And who would you rather have come to your aid when a pipe has broken in your home and water is spewing everywhere: someone who has passed every written test on plumbing for the past year with no experience, or someone who has ridden along and watched and helped out with a plumber for six months on house calls?

Perhaps you think, "Those are skills jobs, and we are educating people." If so, ask yourself, "Aren't we teaching them to be able to do something when they are deemed educated?" What is that thing we are helping them learn how to do? Sometimes one challenge is to make certain we've identified correctly all the things we want them to learn and that we are teaching to the correct learning outcomes. But I think sometimes we misidentify what the actual teaching goals are. We say we want them to learn to identify X number of muscles on a mammal in the lab, but what we really mean is that we want them to learn to work on a team, develop cooperation skills, learn how it feels to cut on something, understand the texture of muscles, and be able to identify the difference in appearance of fat, muscles, and connective tissues. Those are very different outcomes and require a different sort of teaching than simply identifying muscles.

By assigning learners a grade in a course, we are declaring that they have certain skills and knowledge. My question is, Have we accurately assessed those skills we intended to teach?

## Quizzes

If you are going to use quizzes for assessment—and these are appropriate in some situations—it is important to have more than one version of the quiz. Using question alternates works well. I've also found that it's best to prepare a question for every competency and then write question alternates. You can create question sets for each competency such that there are multiple question alternates for each; thus you can give each person a different combination of questions for the test. I like to have at least three alternates for each question. I prefer five, but I learned how time consuming that is. I found that I'd write five alternates for the first five competencies. Then, when I realized time was running out, I'd have to scramble to create only one question for each of the final twenty competencies. Prioritize your tasks based on your own situation.

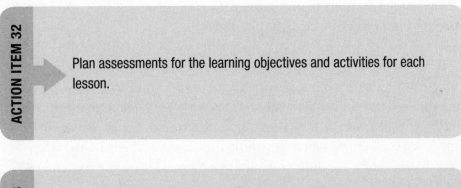

**ACTION ITEM 32**

Plan assessments for the learning objectives and activities for each lesson.

**ACTION ITEM 33**

Create the assessment activities for each lesson.

# Points Earned

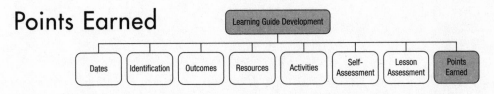

For each Learning Guide, it is important to alert learners to the number of points earned for the assignments in that lesson. If you use the system proposed earlier that makes every course worth 1,000 points, you can very easily document the cumulative number of points that have been possible for each lesson as you progress through the course. For example, if Lesson 3 is worth 150 points and it was possible to earn a total of 200 points on the previous two lessons combined, I would add the following to the bottom of the Learning Guide for Lesson 3:

150 points possible out of 350 points possible so far

650 points remaining possible after this lesson

This allows learners to know where they stand at all times and to self-monitor their progress through the course.

By using the design features proposed in *Conquering the Content*, you will create an environment in which learners are confident of their pathway through the course. This obvious pathway will ensure that the only challenge to learners will be the course content, not course navigation. This focus on learners when designing the course will ensure that the focus of the course for both you and your learners is on the content and not logistics.

Course logistics questions detract from the true reason you are available for your learners: for them to learn information they cannot get from any other source. A properly designed and developed course should trigger very few logistical questions during the semester, so your time can be spent on interacting with learners, Creating robust Learning Guides will facilitate this process. Next we will prioritize features of your course to develop first.

## FACULTY USE OF LEARNING GUIDES

- A composition professor uses one Learning Guide for each of the eight papers learners write during the course.

- A life sciences professor includes vocabulary terms in the Learning Guide so that learners are sure which new terms are introduced in that lesson.

- A math instructor indicates prerequisite knowledge in the Learning Guide so that learners can recognize areas of weakness that may have an impact on the current lesson.

- An education instructor received positive feedback from learners after altering the Learning Guides to include points possible for the lesson and cumulative points possible so far in the course.

- An engineering professor found that Learning Guides reduced learners' questions regarding what was expected.

- An architecture professor uses Learning Guides for a project-based course.

**SHARE**

Share your Learning Guide and view others in the *Conquering the Content* Community: http://ConqueringtheContent.com/LG/Share

# 4

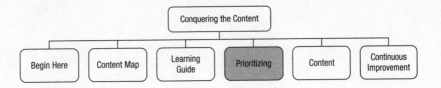

# PRIORITIZING

 HTTP://CONQUERINGTHECONTENT.COM/PRI/INTRO

**Lesson Relevance:** Upon completion of the Content Map and Learning Guides, you have a strong architectural framework for your online course. It is now time to determine the highest-priority items to add next. We will move to layering course features so that at any time you may need to stop development and start delivery, you will have a course that is consistent throughout. With this method of development, you have logical stopping options as you add layers of richness to the course. Even if you run out of time, it will be fine because your course will be polished and purposeful throughout the entire course, though it may not be fully robust yet.

| CONQUERING THE CONTENT: A BLUEPRINT FOR ONLINE COURSE DESIGN AND DEVELOPMENT |
| --- |
| Lesson 4, Prioritizing |

| LEARNING OBJECTIVES | |
| --- | --- |
| Prioritizing | Upon completion of this lesson, you will be able to: |
| | • Rank in priority order the features of your online course to develop. |
| | • Plan sequential improvements to your online course. |
| | • Add layers of richness to your course as time permits. |

| LEARNING RESOURCES | |
| --- | --- |
| References | • Learning Guides developed in Lesson 3. |
| | • Smith, R. "Lesson 3, Learning Guides." *Conquering the Content: A Blueprint for Online Course Design and Development.* San Francisco: Jossey-Bass, 2014. |

| | |
|---|---|
| Required Resource | • Smith, R. "Lesson 4, Prioritizing." *Conquering the Content: A Blueprint for Online Course Design and Development.* San Francisco: Jossey-Bass, 2014. |

**LEARNING ACTIVITIES**

| | |
|---|---|
| Activities for This Lesson | • Rank in priority order the yet to be developed features of your course that will have the greatest impact for learners. |
| | • Rank from shortest to longest the yet to be developed features of your course based on your best guess about how long it will take to complete these portions. |
| | • Plot the learner impact and development time of the remaining items in the course. |
| | • Prioritize the most important features of the course to place online first. |

**SELF-ASSESSMENT**

| | |
|---|---|
| Check Your Understanding | • Selection of the course features with the highest impact on learners. |
| | • Selection of the least time-consuming features of the course. |

**LESSON ASSESSMENT**

| | |
|---|---|
| "Graded" Assessments or Evidence to Proceed | • Prioritized list of the features to develop |

# PRIORITIZE COURSE DEVELOPMENT

Once you have completed Learning Guides for each lesson of your course, take a realistic look at the amount of time you have between now and the beginning of the semester in which you will teach. If you've completed the Action Items up to this point, you've already created both the Content Map and Learning Guides. These two items form a solid structure for your online course.

## Your Next Step

It is now time to determine the next step best suited to your situation.

### Option 1

Depending on the amount of time you have left before classes begin, you may want to stop for now. If that is the case, you will have the opportunity to gather feedback from your learners regarding the helpfulness of the Content Map and Learning Guides. Perhaps you will be teaching a blended or hybrid course and can provide the content in a face-to-face setting. You can pick up with this lesson again when you are ready to add additional features to your online course. This may sound really tempting because you've already accomplished a great deal. However, there may be a few additional things that are not very time consuming that you might also select to include at this time. Please consider Option 2 as well to see if anything from that option might be important to you at this time.

### Option 2

If you are placing your entire course online, we have more work to do. At this point, it will be helpful for you to determine which of the aspects you described in the Learning Guides are the highest-priority features to include. Is it some type of assessment? Content segments? Opportunities for practice? Audio introductions to the lesson? It is best to select features that you can complete for all lessons prior to the beginning of the semester.

It may be that there is no time remaining prior to the beginning of classes, and your goal is simply to stay one or two weeks ahead of your learners. I refer to this as the suicide method of course development. Please do not use this method. You, your family, and your learners will all know this is happening; it will be miserable for you and everyone around you, and it will be a very difficult semester for everyone involved. Instead, if it is an option, perhaps you can take a blended approach, rather than having your course fully online, so that you meet during some class periods and have supplemental materials online.

## Layering

It is essential to set some priorities for the process of creating your online course in case time runs out before the semester begins. I recommend that you develop your priority 1 item for each lesson in the course and *then* move to priority 2 and complete that for each lesson in the course. In this way, you are building layers of richness throughout your course so that you have a consistent course at all times and can stop as needed, rather than spending lots of time on Lesson 1 and then being in a bind to complete Lesson 2 in a short time frame. Next I offer a few suggestions about ways to prioritize the portions of your course on which to focus initially.

# REDUCE LEARNER ANXIETY

Determine which items are important to your learners and include those in your course from the beginning. Making it a priority to reduce potential learner anxiety will substantially benefit both you and the learners. Provide information that will help them be clear about your expectations of them and confident of their standing in your course. The following items are a good place to begin:

- Grades
- Syllabus
- Frequent feedback
- Calendar/schedule of due dates

Prioritizing

Prioritize Course Development

Reduce Learner Anxiety

Consider Learner Needs

Reduce Faculty Anxiety

Select Priorities Blueprint

Teach for the Long Term

- Your contact information
- Your availability times

It is important to let learners know the context of their grade. Horton (2012) recommends providing three pieces of information when releasing grades:

1. The learner's score
2. The passing score
3. What the learner should do next

Here are two examples Horton provided:

- Congratulations. You passed.

  Your score: 85. Passing score: 75

  Continue with the next lesson

- Sorry. You failed.

  Your score: 66. Passing score: 75

  Review the summary and retake the test.

Simple, direct information and next steps help reduce learners' anxiety and give them an action to take in response to the information.

 **TIME-SAVING TIP**

Reducing learner anxiety means reducing your time commitment during the course. If you do not have to answer learner logistics questions, both you and your learners have more time to focus on the content.

# CONSIDER LEARNER NEEDS

When I taught a sophomore-year human anatomy and physiology course, I knew that the only reason the learners were taking the course was that it was a prerequisite for another course. The learners were going to a variety of places after my class—some to professional schools, for example. I understood that my success was really measured by how well those learners were prepared

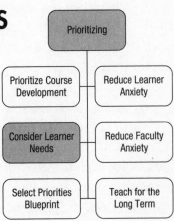

for the next course they were going to take. It was during that next course that they would find out whether I had done them justice or cheated them out of their tuition money and their time investment in my course. So how well they did in my course was not really the issue; much bigger issues were at stake.

I realized that many of the learners did not know how to study, so I began teaching them how. The first thing we did was to take a learning styles inventory to find out how we learned best. Then we began to use that information. Second, I began to show them how to organize their study materials. Third, I gave them all of my notes and slides so they could take notes from my lecture onto the PowerPoint presentation. Fourth, I presented material in small sections of information and reminded them that they could learn as they went about their everyday lives—while waiting for a child to finish a piano lesson, for example. Fifth, I related the new information I was presenting to something with which they were already familiar. We used lots of food analogies—for example, in a nerve, the myelin sheath was the breading around a corn dog, and the axon was the hot dog.

Some learners once suggested that it would be easier to learn the muscles of the cat if they had a video to study by. I asked if they wanted to make the video themselves so that the next group of learners would be able to use it. This gave them an opportunity for active learning and an opportunity to teach other learners, which reinforced their own learning as well. This project in fact taught us many things. In addition to dealing with the technology issues, the learners learned persistence and commitment. When they ran into roadblocks and wanted to quit, I did not allow them to back out of the project. We brainstormed, came up with possible options, and moved ahead. In the end, the learners added music to the demonstration and were extremely proud of their work. (This was 1998, so the project was more difficult than it is today.) Each of the learners wanted a copy of the video to show their families.

The next year, I offered the video to that year's learners, but they had heard about the previous learners making a video and also wanted to create a video and do better than the previous year's learners. So what the first group of learners had originally thought would be a study aid was not the actual aid; the process of producing the aid was the actual aid.

When we know that we are responsible for students' learning, we begin to take the long-term view. In that same course on anatomy and physiology, I had the learners study Latin and Greek prefixes, suffixes, and root words. Understanding the meaning of these terms would give them the ability to determine, at least partially, the meanings of unfamiliar new terms they encountered. This was a skill that would give them an advantage as they progressed in whatever field they chose. All semester, we had weekly quizzes about these terms. In the second semester, we repeated the groups of terms again so that the learners would be revisiting those terms and reviewing and renewing their information. I encountered several learners years later who told me how helpful it was to have learned those Greek and Latin terms and how it had given them such an advantage over the other learners in their courses in professional school.

Another thing we tend to do if we see ourselves as being on the same team with our learners is to give them some of those hints and techniques we've learned over the years to help us recall information. Many of us have insider's secrets to ways to learn and remember, and we sometimes feel obligated to keep those to ourselves so that the learners will "think we're smart." In fact, they already know you're smart, and there is no need to maintain a facade that you are the all-knowing being.

Dissemination of information is no longer limited to faculty members. For example, all of the course work from the Massachusetts Institute of Technology is available on the Internet, and most other information is freely available as well. The way you add value now is very different than it was when you were the keeper of the information. You have become the one who understands what is most important and the best way to problem-solve for your subject matter, and the one who is needed to communicate the concepts behind the facts so that learners can understand them.

In this situation, your goal is to establish a rapport with your learners and to show them that you are on their team and to help them reach their goal. You are not the person standing between them and the goal, trying to keep them from it if they don't do well. Rather than gatekeepers, we are now their encouragers. In my opinion, it is a much more pleasant interaction.

# REDUCE FACULTY ANXIETY

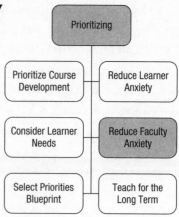

It is essential that you reduce your own anxiety about teaching online and meeting the challenges of something new. I advise that you answer two questions as you begin the process of prioritizing. The first question is, "What irritates me the most about my face-to-face course?" There are many possible answers—for example, "Learners asking for another copy of the syllabus," "Learners asking for test results," "Learners asking for their grade average," or "Learners asking for last week's notes."

Once you've answered the first question, you've identified a priority item to place online first. This often coincides with the items that help reduce learner anxiety. The most irritating thing to me was learners asking me if I had the tests graded, followed by, "What's my grade average now?" In response, I decided to put the exams and grades online first. Learners could see their results immediately following submission of the test, and they were also allowed to see their course average at any time. With the grades online, a learner could check his or her grade repeatedly and never ask me about it a single time. The learners were happy because they were able to look at their grades to their hearts' content, and I was happy because I didn't need to answer repeated questions about grades.

> ⏰ **TIME-SAVING TIP**
>
> Find a colleague or small group to go through *Conquering the Content* with you. The shared experience will be richer, and the social support will make the process more enjoyable. I often find these collaborative experiences help me get to a finished product faster than when I'm working on my own.

The second question is, "What is the most time-consuming aspect of the course for me?" It may be any number of things: grading exams, posting grades, grading discussions, administering exams, giving out handouts, or giving quizzes. Your answer is another priority item to place online.

Often there are efficient ways of dealing with these kinds of issues in an online course. Therefore, what might be extremely time consuming if done manually may become a much faster process if automated electronically.

If you put the most irritating and the most time-consuming aspects of your current course into your online course first, you will have an immediate payoff: a positive outcome from a previously negative experience, and a return on your time investment. With this additional time, you can work on other aspects of your online course.

If you are skeptical about the entire concept of online courses (and it is OK to be skeptical), it is also very important to begin with something that gives you a positive payoff so that you are not investing time in a less rewarding portion of the course at the start. In the end, if it is up to you about which portions of your course to have online and which portions to retain for the face-to-face environment, you will have placed those most helpful to you online and left the other tasks for the face-to-face interactions.

Ideally we would place the knowledge transference portions of the course online and use the face-to-face environment for integrative learning. Learners benefit greatly when they can interact with you and with each other, through discussion and application, to incorporate the content they are learning. Opportunities to learn from you about how to use the concepts will elevate the value of your expertise and therefore learners' time with you. Draves (2002) suggests that cognitive learning is more efficient online than in the face-to-face environment and that integrative learning is more effective in the face-to-face environment when that cognitive learning has taken place online, leaving more time for the communication to occur face-to-face.

# SELECT PRIORITIES BLUEPRINT

If you plan to make six videos for each of the twenty major points of content you've developed and there are only ten weeks between now and the beginning of the semester, you may (wisely) determine that those 120 videos are not going to happen this semester. So it is important for you to find the three most difficult concepts and make videos for only those concepts in the coming weeks. Or if you've planned to develop one case study with a complex story line that ties in concepts from each of the twenty chunks you've developed, you may determine that twenty individual case vignettes would be simpler for you to write.

As I've made clear throughout this book, I consider the Learning Guides a primary item to include. Participants will make a very quick decision about your course based on its organization, and the Learning Guide will go a long way toward keeping your course organized. Prior to making your home page look nice or doing anything else in your course, you need to make sure the content is in order. Whether the course is visually appealing is secondary to the need for the learning principles to be in place. The first impression will matter, but after that, learners want to log in, get to the course materials, get their work finished, and move on to another part of their life. Most are not looking to you for their most impressive encounter with graphic design.

As previously mentioned, developing one item for the entire course and then adding an additional feature for the entire course ensures uniformity throughout the course. Also, it is best not to spend an inordinate amount of time on the colors of the home page, your slides, and other online material. Most programs have templates designed by graphic artists with training in color coordination. Typically we instructors can't do a lot better than they have. We will be more effective pouring our creativity and energy into our teaching rather than into color alterations.

## Selecting Your Specific Priorities

It is now time to determine what you see as the highest-priority items to develop first. In Action Items 34 and 35, you are going to employ two different perspectives (impact and ease of completion) to rank the items to include next. You will then make a decision about how to proceed.

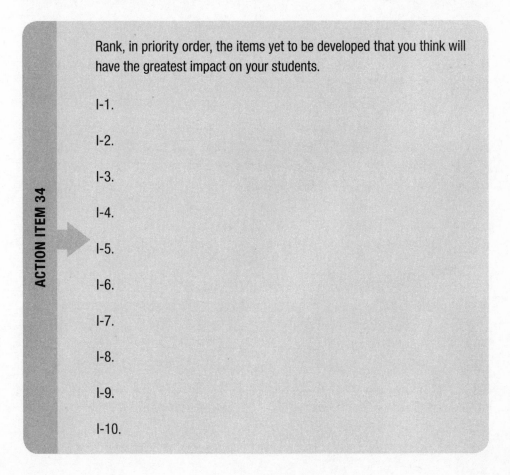

**ACTION ITEM 34**

Rank, in priority order, the items yet to be developed that you think will have the greatest impact on your students.

I-1.

I-2.

I-3.

I-4.

I-5.

I-6.

I-7.

I-8.

I-9.

I-10.

Rank, in priority order, the items yet to be developed that you think will take the least amount of time to develop.

T-1.

T-2.

T-3.

T-4.

T-5.

T-6.

T-7.

T-8.

T-9.

T-10.

Plot the items from the two lists you created in Action Items 34 and 35 into the four quadrants.

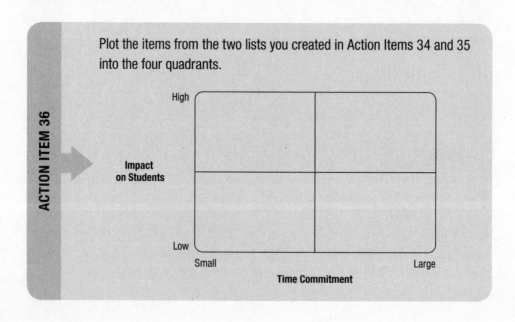

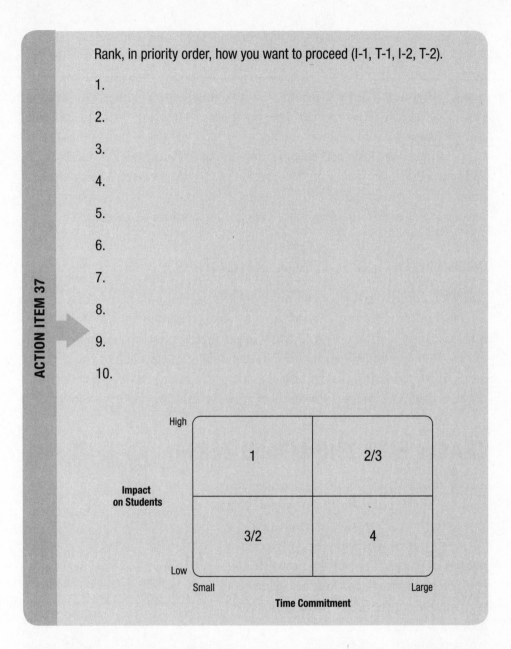

Rank, in priority order, how you want to proceed (I-1, T-1, I-2, T-2).

**ACTION ITEM 37**

1.

2.

3.

4.

5.

6.

7.

8.

9.

10.

Depending on the amount of time you have left as well as other priorities you have, what is the wisest choice from here? Do any items have high impact and small time commitment? These items are priority 1. Save the low-impact, large-time-commitment items until after everything else is completed (priority 4).

Next you need to choose between high-impact, large-time-commitment and low-impact, small-time-commitment items. Whether each of these is priority 2 or priority 3 for you will depend on how big of an impact they have and how much time you have to devote to completing them. You might be able to develop three low-impact, small-time-commitment items in the same amount of time that you could develop one high-impact, large-time-commitment item. Do the three items together have the same impact as the one? It's your choice and best wisdom at this point. Because you've already completed the highest-impact items, you probably can't go wrong at this point, so don't stress over the selection; just jump in so that you get something additional completed.

## Moving Through the Priorities

Now that you have developed your priority list, you will know what to do next whenever you have a bit of time to work on something. We hope you have some extra time now and can work through a few layers. Refer back to Lesson 3 (Learning Guide) for details on developing each of the components of the Learning Guide, or to Lesson 5 (Content) to develop specific presentations of concepts for learners. You are making awesome progress!

# TEACH FOR THE LONG TERM

As you move forward with developing your content, please consider this question: What if you knew your learners were going to be tested six months following the completion of your course, and you would be compensated based on their retention of your course content? How would you teach differently?

Would you

- Reduce the amount of material you cover?

- Make sure you don't overload the learners with extraneous information?

- Give the information in a format compatible with their learning modes?

- Ask them what format is the most helpful to their learning?

- Not care how they received the information, so long as they learned it?

- Not care if they were coming to class or staying home, so long as they were learning the material and giving feedback that they were learning?

- Care about the "copyright" of your lectures if you were held liable for the future performance of your learners?

- Provide practice opportunities?

How much attention would you pay to your presentation under these circumstances?

- Would you prepare in advance?

- Would you change the quiz questions?

- Would you change the way you spent time during class?

- What sort of handouts and other learning aids would you offer?

- What would you want to know about your learners before you began teaching them?
  - That they know how to study?
  - That they know how they learn best?
  - That they know the best study and learning methods for them?

- Would your convenience be a factor in your teaching, or would their learning be at the center of your concern?

- Would you be concerned about corralling them into a large group so that you have to lecture only one time?

In this situation, here is what I would probably want to do:

- Check individually with each learner to make sure that each person is understanding the concepts.

- Make sure that each learner understands the concepts in terms of both comprehension and application.

- Know what each learner's weaknesses are so that I could invoke measures to support and correct those weaknesses.

- Get frequent feedback from them about how the course was going.

- Find out how they are understanding the material and whether the course needs any changes in order for them to comprehend things better.

- Find out as early as possible whether they are learning and retaining the material, and not wait until very far into the semester to verify.

- Make certain they understand the material, apply it to as many different situations as possible, have as much practice as needed, and integrate it into their everyday world and existing knowledge.

- Refer to previous information in each subsequent module and relate each concept to each of the other concepts, making certain the learners understand the context for each concept, the big picture, and how everything fits together.

If we know that these are the ways we would go about things if we had to make sure the learners still knew the content six months later, why don't we just make those changes now? I think my content is important enough for them to remember it in six months, and undoubtedly you feel that way about yours. In some cases, it is important for learners to be able to retain the content over the course of their whole career, so it seems imperative that we take decisive measures to ensure we are teaching in such a way that learners retain the information for the long term. If the information we are teaching is not important enough for them to remember six months from now, then perhaps we should reexamine our content and find some more lasting ideas on which to spend our time and theirs in the course.

## FACULTY EXPERIENCES WITH PRIORITIZING AND LAYERING

- A faculty member uncertain about teaching online used layering to gradually increase portions of his course that were online so that the online component advanced from supplemental to fully online. Positive learner feedback and allowing himself time to become more comfortable with the online environment were the keys to success.

- A reluctant humanities professor became interested and motivated to move additional components of the course to the online environment when an opportunity for international travel arose during the semester.

- An elementary education professor is using prioritizing and layering to help future teachers learn to teach online.

SHARE

Share your Prioritizing ideas and view others in the *Conquering the Content* Community: http://ConqueringtheContent.com/PRI/Share

# 5

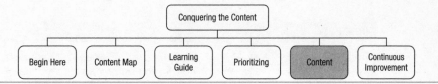

Conquering the Content

Begin Here | Content Map | Learning Guide | Prioritizing | Content | Continuous Improvement

# CONTENT

**PLAY AUDIO INTRODUCTION** ▶ HTTP://CONQUERINGTHECONTENT.COM/CO/INTRO

**Lesson Relevance:** Presenting content according to what we know about how people learn will help your learners accomplish their goals. Chunking course content into absorbable pieces of information and reinforcing those chunks with learning activities will help learners move the content from working memory into long-term storage. This lesson offers guidelines for chunking your content and creating bridges of transition from one chunk to the next.

---

**CONQUERING THE CONTENT: A BLUEPRINT FOR ONLINE COURSE DESIGN AND DEVELOPMENT**

Lesson 5, Content

---

### LEARNING OBJECTIVES

Content

Upon completion of this lesson, you will be able to:

- Recognize the benefits of chunking course content.
- Apply the steps to chunking content.
- Create bridges (transitions) between content chunks.
- Reinforce content chunks with learning activities.

---

### LEARNING RESOURCES

References

- Clark, R. C., Nguyen, F., and Sweller, J. *Efficiency in Learning: Evidence-Based Guidelines to Manage Cognitive Load.* San Francisco: Jossey-Bass/Pfeiffer, 2006.
- SoftChalk Lesson Builder (http://www.softchalk.com/).
- Respondus StudyMate (http://www.respondus.com/products/studymate.shtml).

| LEARNING ACTIVITIES | |
|---|---|
| Activities for This Lesson | • Complete Felder and Soloman's Index of Learning Styles Questionnaire: http://www.engr.ncsu.edu/learningstyles/ilsweb.htm. |
| | • Identify concepts to be used in chunks for one of your lessons. |
| | • Develop introduction, content chunks, learning activities, and transition statements for one of your lessons. |
| | • Chunk course content into absorbable pieces of information. |
| | • Create bridges. |

| SELF-ASSESSMENT | |
|---|---|
| Check Your Understanding | • Divide major points of course competencies into five- to seven-minute segments. |
| | • Be able to create bridges between content chunks. |

| LESSON ASSESSMENT | |
|---|---|
| "Graded" Assessments or Evidence to Proceed | • Create content chunks for course materials in each lesson. |
| | • Create introductions, reviews, and bridges for chunks in each lesson. |

# HOW YOU LEARN

Although there is debate about the effectiveness and validity of the concept of learning styles, finding out about them has changed the way I teach by making me more open to multiple ways of learning. When I first began to teach, I thought everyone learned the way I do: by taking notes and reorganizing the information into different configurations until I know and understand it from several different angles. Discovering that my way of learning is not everyone's approach was very eye-opening for me.

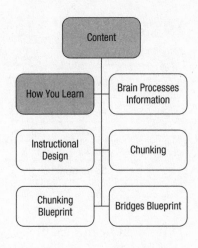

My experience with individuals in my classes highlighted the need for flexible learning experiences. A learner in one of my face-to-face courses was failing the lab exams. Spelling counted in these exams, because in anatomy, the change of one letter in a word can give it a totally different meaning. She also could not pronounce the words correctly, and I was continually trying to help her with her pronunciation. We came up with a solution: I recorded the lab words for her. I repeated each word slowly three times before I moved to the next one. Once I finished the list that way, I went back through the entire list saying each word one time and asking her to repeat the word after me, this time pausing long enough in the recording for her to do so. She used the recording to practice while doing other things in her life. On the next lab exam, she earned a 98 percent. We both were elated at her success! I made a recording for her for each of the remaining exams. Perhaps you are thinking, "Yes, but that takes too much time!" It does take time, but in the whole scheme of things, those few minutes I spent each week were well worth my time to accommodate her learning needs. I had just assisted a learner to be successful in a very difficult course. These are the rewarding moments of teaching—I'm so glad I didn't miss that one! In addition, my time investment for that individual made the same option available to others as well: once I created the recordings, they were available for any other learner who might want to use them.

An exercise that I find useful in helping faculty imagine additional ways to present content is to take this learning inventory. (See page 110.)

ACTION ITEM 38

Take Felder and Soloman's Index of Learning Styles Questionnaire (http://www.engr.ncsu.edu/learningstyles/ilsweb.html) and record your scores along the continua.

| Perceiving | 11 | 9 | 7 | 5 | 3 | 1 | 1 | 3 | 5 | 7 | 9 | 11 | Intuitive |
|---|---|---|---|---|---|---|---|---|---|---|---|---|---|
| Visual | 11 | 9 | 7 | 5 | 3 | 1 | 1 | 3 | 5 | 7 | 9 | 11 | Auditory |
| Active | 11 | 9 | 7 | 5 | 3 | 1 | 1 | 3 | 5 | 7 | 9 | 11 | Reflective |
| Sequential | 11 | 9 | 7 | 5 | 3 | 1 | 1 | 3 | 5 | 7 | 9 | 11 | Global |

It might be informative to have your students take this index of learning styles. There are many good general hints about studying available to students from the results page after completing the index. Regardless of how you process information, it is helpful to be aware that people can learn in very different ways, and providing some flexibility for your students can make a big difference.

A study by Felder (1993) addresses global and sequential information processing. Those individuals who process information globally are skilled at viewing issues at the "big picture" level. Those who process sequentially usually proceed stepwise through the information, considering individual details prior to understanding the big picture. The "Index of Learning Styles" website (Felder and Soloman, n.d.) provides several ways to help faculty address different learning styles. In particular, faculty seldom give the big picture of what they are teaching prior to delving into the details. Nevertheless, it is important for global learners that we present the global picture at the beginning (just as I outlined in the Preface what this book is about) and connect what the learners are about to encounter with some subjects with which they are already familiar. This process allows learners to frame the new knowledge in its proper context. Many teachers are perceivers, meaning that they need information to come in through the five senses and in a sequential manner, so they may tend to teach that way. Intuitive learners learn in "fits and starts." They may get the answer, but cannot explain where or how they did it. At times these individuals can be accused of cheating because they cannot identify the steps to working out a problem, even though they know the correct answer. It takes them a while to discern how they arrive at what it is they know.

Sheila Tobias's research (1991) on learners who set out to be science majors and changed their major after the first year highlights the issues related to sequential and global information processing. Science courses at the time she did her research were frequently taught sequentially, without providing a global overview. She found that the overwhelming number of those who changed their major were global learners.

Look back at what you wrote about your favorite teacher. Did this person make a special effort to relate to the learners? Did the person take a special interest in you? Many times that is the case. Most of us decided to teach so that we could make a difference in people's lives. But when the opportunity arises, sometimes we tend to shrink back because of time constraints. Let us not rob ourselves of the rewards of our profession for lack of time! Most of us are successful because someone took the time to take a special interest in us and invest extra time in our lives.

Felder (1988, p. 675) defines teaching style in terms of answers to five questions:

1. What types of information does the instructor emphasize: concrete (factual) or abstract (conceptual, theoretical)?

2. What mode of presentation is stressed: visual (pictures, diagrams, films, demonstrations) or verbal (lectures, readings, discussions)?

3. How is the presentation organized: inductively (phenomena leading to principles) or deductively (principles leading to phenomena)?

4. What mode of learner participation does the presentation facilitate: active (students talk, move, reflect) or passive (students watch and listen)?

5. What type of perspective is provided on the information presented: sequential (step-by-step progression—the trees) or global (context and relevance—the forest)?

These questions are important to consider when creating content for your learners.

Most of us have had more experience with the face-to-face environment and have had modeled for us ways to present content in these circumstances. How should we do this in an online environment? Some faculty choose to record themselves lecturing in a face-to-face setting. This has some limited benefit. If the purpose is to review and to catch up on a missed class, this might be a reasonable solution. However, if a course is fully online, it seems that a recorded lecture from a face-to-face class sends the message that you didn't want to create something specific for this new format. It would be similar to generating a transcript of a presentation you gave at a conference and calling it a journal article. The two learning environments are very different and thus require a different product if we are to offer the best experience to the participants.

# HOW THE BRAIN PROCESSES INFORMATION

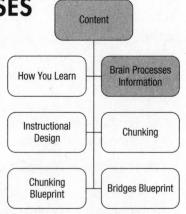

It is important to ensure that we present content in a way that maximizes the focus on the learning goal and the opportunity for learners to comprehend the subject as well as prepare them to later retrieve the information. Activating prior learning helps place the new information in the context of what is already known. Ensuring that the focus of learning activities is directly on the current learning objective allows learners to focus their efforts on the specific goal. Creating content in a way that allows learners flexibility will aid their progress through the content.

## Organization of Prior Learning

Experts employ schema that enable the working memory to function much more efficiently. Clark, Nguyen, and Sweller (2006) refer to the process of using schema as automaticity; it can allow us to largely bypass the limits of working memory. Novices do not have these schema and therefore need structures within the learning environment to substitute for schema in processing information. For example, if I say, "Each of the mammals in North America is found in the Cincinnati Zoo," I am assuming some prior knowledge that my learners may or may not possess. In order to understand my statement, learners have to know this information:

- What mammals are
- What countries are in North America
- Where Cincinnati is
- Whether Cincinnati is a city, county, or state
- What a zoo is

Anyone who knows this information will consider my sentence a very simple one, but anyone lacking this information will find this sentence and any other information on the topic difficult to understand.

Next, I'll give an example that will be more difficult to follow because you are likely unfamiliar with it. If I say, "The pronotal expansion in *Gargaphia* is typically more open than that of *Leptopharsa*." Prior knowledge required here includes the following:

- What a pronotal expansion is
- What *Gargaphia* is (or are)
- What "more open" means
- What *Leptopharsa* is (or are)

Then I proceed to tell you that this is because the cells in *Gargaphia* are generally larger in diameter than those of *Leptopharsa*, and the cell margins in *Gargaphia* are typically thinner than those of *Leptopharsa*. Are you continuing to follow my line of thinking? Most likely not, in particular if you hear this information and have no knowledge of how to spell *Gargaphia* or *Leptopharsa* and if I am giving you no visual images of either of these organisms (they are insects) or the parts of their anatomy to which I am referring. You can see how difficult it is for a novice to follow along when information is not clear.

To promote understanding, I should have an image of *Gargaphia* and *Leptopharsa*, be able to show where a pronotum is and what the pronotal expansion is, and be able to show a comparison of larger and smaller cells and thick and thin cell margins.

Information-processing theories assume that individuals have a limited working memory, and when it is overloaded, no learning will take place. Primarily it is the learner's prior knowledge that determines how much information can be held simultaneously in working memory. In general, the less prior knowledge a learner has, the more prone he or she is to cognitive overload (Cook, 2006). For example, graduate learners can learn with more complex interactions.

## Cognitive Load

Cognitive load theory is a universal set of learning principles that have been proven to result in efficient instructional environments by leveraging human cognitive learning processes. We need to take three main types of cognitive load into consideration in order to minimize wasteful forms of cognitive load and maximize the useful forms (Clark, Nguyen, and Sweller, 2006):

- Intrinsic load. This is mental work imposed by the complexity of the content and determined by your instructional goals. Complex tasks, which involve coordination in the memory, are more complex than a series of calculations or memory exercises.

- Germane load. This is mental work imposed by instructional activities that benefit the instructional goal.

- Extraneous load. This is mental work that is irrelevant to the learning goal and consequently wastes limited mental resources and drains mental capacity.

To create efficient instruction, we need to maximize germane load and minimize extraneous load. Although you usually cannot control the intrinsic load associated with the learning goals, you can manage it by segmenting and sequencing content in ways that optimize the amount of element interactivity required at any one time (Clark, Nguyen, and Sweller, 2006).

# Qualities of Online Content

In an online course, both the learners and the faculty member are interacting via the content online, so it is helpful to modify the content specifically for this environment. First we need to identify some important qualities of this online content. As mentioned previously, here are four requirements you should consider:

| QUALITY | DESCRIPTION |
|---|---|
| Chunk-ability | Ability to move through the content in short, directed learning segments |
| Repeat-ability | Ability to repeat and review content |
| Pause-ability | Ability to stop and resume without having to start all over |
| Understand-ability | Ability to be clearly understood because of direct instructions |

Regardless of the medium used to deliver content, these are good qualities to keep in mind.

In Lesson 1, Begin Here, I noted that online learning is different from face-to-face learning because of the environment. In an online environment, learners are no longer surrounded by a room full of other learners who are all focused on the same subject for fifty minutes of protected time. Instead, interruptions become part of the expectations of online learning, and they require your course content to have the four characteristics.

## Chunk-ability

Chunks are short, directed learning segments. Chunking is grouping pieces of information into meaningful segments. If your content is chunked, it is divided into short segments of passive learning, followed by an opportunity for active learning on those same concepts to reinforce the principle just introduced.

## Repeat-ability

This concept refers to the ability to repeat and review content. Learners need the option to replay segments of presentations so that they can review content. Repetition of content helps move information from short-term memory into long-term memory (Clark, Nguyen, and Sweller, 2006). It is important to be able to replay a small portion of a presentation for clarification purposes without having to listen to the entire presentation.

## Pause-ability

This refers to the ability to stop and resume without having to start all over. Some interruptions can be taken care of quickly, and the learner is back to the presentation almost right away, but those few seconds of a presentation may have been crucial. It is better for the learner to be able to pause and hear everything you are saying than to have to start from the beginning in order to get just a few words. Chances are that the learner will not have time to come back to that presentation again just for a few words. Adding a pause option increases the likelihood that learners will absorb all of the content (Reiser and Dempsey, 2012).

## Understand-ability

Clear, direct instructions exhibit understand-ability. Instructions in the online environment have to be explicit. Learners can misinterpret or misunderstand things or perceive the tone differently than you intended. You've probably experienced this through miscommunications with emails. It is very important for the sake of your own time management that the instructions in your course are easy to follow. Then you won't be answering logistical questions during the semester when you could be spending your time interacting with the learners about the content. As we saw in Lesson 3, use of Learning Guides will assist you in developing clear, direct instructions.

In order for your content to have these four characteristics, you will have to modify your existing course materials. First, whereas in the face-to-face environment, generally the main focus is on the teacher, in an online course, the main focus is on the content. Now you will design the content to include directives about how to proceed, when to move to specific activities, when to interact with other learners, and other prompts. Whereas in the face-to-face environment you could have directed these activities on the fly, you now have to plan them out in advance and incorporate them into the content.

Second, in an online environment, you have to focus on creating opportunities for interaction among the learners. Giving a topic and instructing learners to discuss it is insufficient to generate a robust discussion. In an asynchronous (not all together at the same time) situation, it is important to give some specifics about what to discuss. For example, in a face-to-face environment, if we ask students to discuss without giving them a specific question to discuss, it's highly likely that the discussion will be off topic and likely unrelated to the subject matter. The same concept applies to discussion questions online. It is important to give the learners something concrete to discuss—for example, "Choose to either support or oppose continued teaching of cursive writing, and give two reasons for your chosen stance."

# INSTRUCTIONAL DESIGN CONSIDERATIONS

When designing and developing the individual chunks of content in your course, you will find it helpful to keep a few instructional design principles in mind.

```
                          Content

How You Learn         Brain Processes
                      Information

Instructional         Chunking
Design

Chunking              Bridges Blueprint
Blueprint
```

## Dual-Mode Effect

Visual information and verbal information are processed in independent portions of the working memory, so these do not compete with each other. Therefore, presentations that take advantage of both the visual (graphics) and the verbal (text or audio) are more beneficial than those that use only one of them (Cook, 2006). This also explains why it is not useful to have a text slide that you read to the learners: both the slide and your words present verbal information that is processed in the same way, so you are not giving any additional information. A better approach would be to present a graphical representation of some element of the content and an audio narration over that graphic.

## Split-Attention Effect

When the design of the graphic does not foster the coordination of visual and verbal material, integration can be difficult because the learner's attention is split between the two modes of information. This process of integration imposes a heavy extraneous cognitive load for novice learners, especially when the material is highly detailed and requires the learner to coordinate many labels with graphical information.

One way to reduce the cognitive load induced by the search for a graphical element referenced in the verbal information is to present related material contiguously in space and time (Wu and Shah, 2004). When material is presented in this way, learners are better able to form associations between the visual and verbal elements (Chandler and Sweller, 1992). Therefore, placing the text explanation on the drawings or having a mouse-over explanation is helpful. Another way to reduce search time is to color-code related graphical and textual elements (Kalyuga, Chandler, and Sweller, 1999).

## Modality Principle

This principle holds that an audio explanation of visuals leads to better learning than a text explanation of visuals (Clark, Nguyen, and Sweller, 2006). This can be accomplished by adding narration to graphics, or audio files to slide presentations.

Research indicates that presenting verbal information in spoken form rather than written form is more likely to increase the capacity of working memory. As for visual information, the use of static graphics rather than animations tends to enhance learning except when representing motion or trajectory (Cook, 2006).

## Presentation Length

A recent study by Pomales-Garcia and Liu (2006) asked participants to watch content modules. They could complete the module, return later and finish a module, or quit and not complete the module. As module length increased from seven to twenty minutes, completion rates went down, and pause and quit rates increased. These results suggest that quitting, pausing, or completing an online module in one session has more to do with the length of the module than with the format (text, audio, or video) in which the module is delivered. As mentioned earlier, segmenting the content into five- to seven-minute chunks has many advantages for both you and the learners.

# Presentation of Information

Using the breaks between short segments as an opportunity to reinforce the concept just presented will allow the learner to initiate the process of reassociating that information with previous knowledge, recalling the new information again, and giving the brain a chance to begin to make connections for storing that information in long-term memory. Sometimes I think of this as sort of like brushing my teeth; one dainty swipe of the toothbrush is not going to remove all of those germs, particularly if I've eaten lots of sweets (crowded my brain with lots of competing information) or if I haven't brushed in a while (it's been a long time since I've heard those concepts). The more brushstrokes I can give at once, the better (up to a point). What is even better is if I brush my teeth twice a day. Brushing them more often will keep them cleaner than if I wait an entire week and brush them for twenty minutes all at once. They might look clean that one day, but three days later, they're not going to look clean no matter how long I brushed them three days ago.

In addition to presenting small segments of learning, varying the processes of instruction so that there is a variety of types of interaction with the content is helpful to learners. Sometimes, for intensive courses a change in the process of instruction may work as well as a break or a rest (Wlodkowski and Ginsberg, 2010).

# Using Knowledge of Brain Processing

When you have a lot of information, you have to address that information frequently at small intervals so that things will not begin to fall through the cracks. Therefore, dividing the learning into short segments followed by active learning opportunities allows learners to absorb and reinforce content in frequent sessions, which is more beneficial than long segments.

One of the most important things you can do is verbalize your thinking process for your learners. Learning your reasoning process and how you process information in your discipline is very important. This is one of those things that must be learned from a mentor. Demonstrating these thinking paths is a major contribution you can make in developing learners.

It is also important to have learners verbalize their thinking back to you so that you will have an opportunity to correct their reasoning processes as they form. Creating a safe environment for this process is one of the responsibilities of faculty members. You can create this safe place in an online course by providing learners with an option to write in a journal or blog, or you can develop a self-reflection component for your course. Having learners think about their thinking (metacognition) reinforces the concepts being covered and thus builds in repetition of information, which is going to strengthen their learning.

## Instructional Guidance

Instructional guidance plays an important role in learning from visual representations, particularly when learning requires active construction of knowledge. Sometimes the free exploration of multimedia presentations can impose a heavy cognitive load (Cook, 2006).

Often multimedia materials are available that are far superior to anything we have the time or the expertise to create. I encourage you to use those whenever possible so that you are not spending your development time recreating something that already exists. It would be better to address any gaps or holes in the existing material. However, when you send learners to the website of a publisher or another website where a video or animation is available, offer them a framework and some guidance. For example, you can explain what they will be viewing and the key points to watch for, and let them know if there are specific segments of great significance. You might say something like, "Watch for the yellow circle representing the neurotransmitter to be released from the dendrite [nerve ending]."

# Feedback

Keep in mind one of Chickering and Gamson's principles of good teaching (1987): offer frequent feedback. If you typically use just a midterm and final exam, it's time to start incorporating more frequent assessments so that learners can benefit from the early intervention and have a greater opportunity to improve their performance.

A recent real-life example of this made me recognize the impact of immediate feedback on my own behavior. The street near the entrance to my institution has a speed limit, which I must admit I had never noticed previously, of only 25 mph. They installed one of those electronic signs that shows you what your current speed is next to the speed limit sign. This *immediately* made a difference to me and the other drivers. When I was given immediate feedback about my performance as it related to the standard (speed limit), I slowed to the speed limit. I thought I'd learned my lesson and would never go over 25 mph again. However, as soon as the digital feedback sign was removed, I was no longer monitoring my own performance, so I must confess that I started speeding again.

 **TIME-SAVING TIP**

Many learning management systems have multiple options to automate feedback throughout their tools. Take advantage of these opportunities to let learners read your friendly acknowledgment of their submissions.

Rubrics are one opportunity for learners to monitor their performance. Another is to offer examples of work. On assignments, do you provide samples of appropriate performance for learners? Samples of excellent, satisfactory, and poor work with annotated explanations of what makes each sample worthy of the grade received can really help learners rise to the level of your expectations for course work.

# CHUNKING

In this section, we will cover the research behind chunking, the many benefits of chunking course content, a demonstration of chunking, and a quick way to evaluate the effectiveness of chunking.

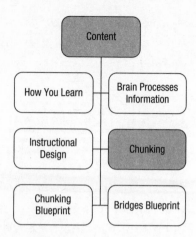

## Introduction

George Miller, a Harvard University psychologist, experimented in 1956 to determine the capacity of human working memory. He found that when given a list of unrelated items, a typical adult can recall between five and nine of them. Forty years later, Garrison, Anderson, and Archer (2001) found that "chunking the content into absorbable pieces helped keep learners from feeling overwhelmed and provided them with the essential information for completing the exercises and grasping the concepts without exhausting them with too much written content" (p. 7). This also relates to creating schemata or scaffolding by which to recall information, which we address later. First let's compare information that is not chunked to that which is.

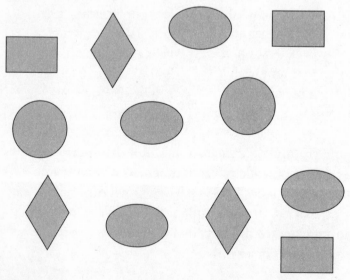

**Figure 5.1**

# Demonstration

View Figure 5.1 for three seconds. Then cover it with a plain piece of paper, and draw on another piece of paper what you remember seeing.

Look at Figure 5.2 for three seconds, cover it with a plain piece of paper, and draw on another piece of paper what you remember seeing.

How did you do? Did you recall more on the second one? Look back at the two images. The only difference was the arrangement of the items.

You weren't viewing different content in these two images, only different arrangements of content. So when we chunk, we aren't asking learners to comprehend anything less; we are only grouping the content into meaningful segments. We still expect them to retain all the same information, but it has been placed into absorbable portions of information.

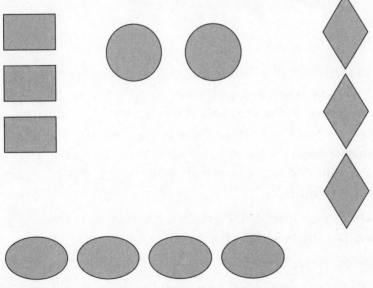

Figure 5.2

Let's try another example of chunking. Look at Figure 5.3 for three seconds, cover it with a piece of paper, and draw what you remember on another piece of paper.

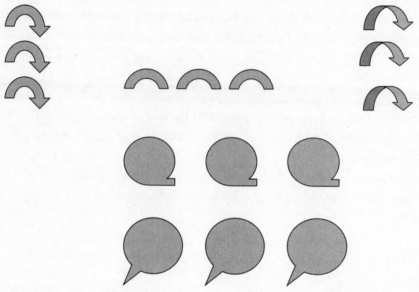

**Figure 5.3**

Was it easier to remember than Figure 5.1 because the images were chunked? I think this one is still pretty difficult.

The information you are presenting to learners is typically totally new to them. They are often learning new vocabulary, new concepts, and new hierarchical arrangements of the information all at the same time in your course, and it can be difficult for them to make sense of any of it.

Let's look again at Figure 5.3.

- Which are more closely related: (1) the two types of arrows or (2) the blunt-ended half-circles and the half-circles with arrows?

- Are the balloons or "call-out shapes" all related to each other?

- Should all the things with points be grouped together and all the objects with blunt ends grouped in a different category?

- If they are organized by blunt versus pointed, some objects fit both categories, so what do you do with them?

Now think of the figure as an analogy for your own content. These types of questions will be in learners' minds as you present your own subject matter because they don't know the content as you do. They wouldn't even know what names to call these objects (I don't either). There is much information to be communicated in the original slide.

In the last figure, although the information has been chunked, there is still a lot of processing that needs to happen with that presentation of the image. A single image may turn out to take several minutes of explanation and further time for reflection on the learners' part. So it is with your content. Even though your presentation may be five to nine minutes long, it will typically take anywhere from two to four times as long for the learners to grasp or process the content. So a five-minute presentation can turn into a ten- or twenty-minute one for the learners by the time they take notes and comprehend what you are presenting. The length of viewing the presentation will fall back to the original five minutes after they learn the concepts and are using the presentation simply for review.

# Benefits

Chunking has these benefits:

- Increased retention and understanding will result.
- Accessing course materials will be more convenient.
- Learners may cover more material.
- Results are measurable.
- Comprehension may be greater.

Miller's rule about adults being able to remember seven plus or minus two items has bearing for adult learning. Content presented in one long segment is much less effective for learning than the same content broken down into several smaller segments. Pomales-Garcia and Liu (2006) found that as module length increased from seven minutes to fourteen and then to twenty-one, learners were less likely to complete the modules.

Presenting your course content as chunks offers learners a number of advantages:

- If learners know they can get something done in twenty minutes, they are more likely to log in when they have that amount of time.

- A learner who logs in to the course more frequently is more likely to keep up.

- If your instructions are clear, concise, and easy to find, your course will be more pleasant for learners to deal with, and they will therefore be less likely to put it off.

- The course will more likely be up-to-date because you will be able to add to and update your course in modular components.

- Learners with an available thirty minutes to study will choose your chunked course over other courses that aren't chunked.

- For learners who prefer to view longer segments, all the material is there, and they can work on one segment after the other without a break. Presenting content in this manner provides options for learners with a variety of needs. They are able to self-select the amount of content they are prepared to take in at one sitting.

## Effectiveness

Once you have experimented with chunking in your online course, you will want to evaluate its effectiveness by getting some feedback from your learners. If you have presented chunked content early in the term, you may not want to wait until the end of the term to find out what your students think. Your institution or department may have standardized evaluations, but a short questionnaire of two to five questions can elicit learners' reaction to changes in the course and give you instant feedback about the effectiveness of the change in the length of presentations.

## CHUNKING BLUEPRINT

Throughout this book, I've been guiding you toward this task of chunking your content, but I have not brought it to your attention until now. If you have already completed the Course Outline (Form 7/8) and Content Map (if you haven't, do so now before continuing), chunking the content will be simple. The process I set out here will work regardless of the subject matter you are teaching.

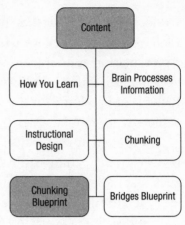

I began teaching this way in the face-to-face environment when I wanted my learners to work their studying into their everyday lives. I would present the information in small bits and encourage them to review it while they were in line somewhere or waiting for an appointment, or at other times when they had a few spare minutes. It proved to be very successful for them.

## The Chunking Process

Chickering and Gamson (1987) document that spending time on task and interacting with the content are important ways to facilitate learning, so it is our job to assist learners through the content. Our challenge is to guide them through the content but still create active learning opportunities for them. As I mentioned earlier, in order to accommodate memory processing, it is best to present five to nine minutes of passive learning followed by a participatory learning activity that will reinforce the concept. We can do this in any number of ways.

First, it will be helpful to identify the learning segments (chunks) by documenting the concept and the reinforcement activity that will help seal this content in the minds of the learners. Then you will place the introduction and transition statements between the chunks. On the Course Outline, you listed the major points you plan to cover in this topic. We'll now expand those to create chunks and bridges.

If you have a slide presentation that you normally show in your face-to-face course as you lecture, you can use portions of the same presentation to create the chunked course content. You just need to alter it a bit to be suitable for online learning. There are several compression utilities that reduce the file size for slide presentations. In addition, there are options for speeding up the playback speed so that learners can listen and watch a presentation at double or more the original recoded speed. These can be very helpful options for busy learners. You might also want to provide a PDF file of handouts for the slide presentation, which gives learners a convenient place to take notes.

There are natural breaks in virtually all presentations. A transition between topics, change of focus, or difference in hierarchy levels are all cues that indicate natural breaks. In general, you can find these breaks every ten to twelve slides; we call these chunks. This is not a hard-and-fast rule, and segments vary in length. You may find that your content naturally falls into a different pattern of lengths. Take one presentation and find these breaks (electronically or on paper). These will serve as content for your chunks from Form 40 (on page 130).

Here is an illustration of how an original slide presentation was revised to create a chunked presentation with three chunks. Notice that bridges are placed between the chunks and that each chunk is sealed with a learning activity. The idea is to surround each of those concepts with an introduction and reinforcement activity plus a transition to the next concept. This gives each concept some context so that it is not an isolated idea; learners gain some understanding of how all the concepts are interrelated.

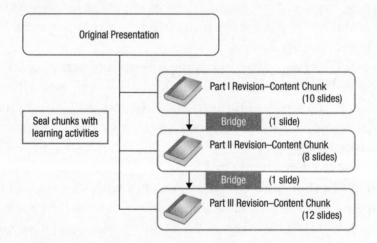

Using your Content Map as a guide, identify concepts to be used as chunks for one of your lessons.

Identify introduction, content chunks, learning activities, and bridges for one of your lessons.

After you complete the Chunks and Bridges form (Form 40), look at the material left over, as you have extracted these major concepts from your lecture. Ask yourself what value is added by that leftover content. If your arch enemy on campus could justify to you that there are pedagogical reasons to use this material in his or her course, then use it. If not, perhaps you need to question why you feel the need to leave it in.

## Chunking for Text-Based Content

For text-based information, you will need to include some visuals to tell learners where they are in the process. As mentioned in Lesson 2, anchor the information with a scaffold of five to nine concepts; within each concept, have five to nine key points; and within each key point, have a number of facts or major points. Make sure that learners always know where you are in that scaffolding so that they are not lost. This is easy to do: use short pages that group together, are linked back to the beginning, are illustrated with a flowchart, or have a tabbing structure to which the learners may refer.

## CHUNKS AND BRIDGES

| OUTCOME/CONCEPT | ELEMENT | DESCRIPTION |
|---|---|---|
| Outcome/Concept 1 | Introduction | |
| | Content chunk | |
| | Learning activity | |
| | Bridge | |
| Outcome/Concept 2 | Introduction | |
| | Content chunk | |
| | Learning activity | |
| | Bridge | |
| Outcome/Concept 3 | Introduction | |
| | Content chunk | |
| | Learning activity | |
| | Bridge | |

Form available at www.josseybass.com/go/conqueringthecontent

It is best not to have learners scroll down the screens; a better choice is to have multiple pages that learners click through. After a major concept is presented and illustrated, learners need an opportunity to interact with that content in an active way in order to reinforce the concept in their mind.

# BRIDGES BLUEPRINT

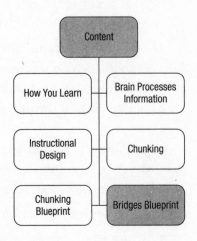

Bridges assist in transitioning from one chunk of content to the next. A bridge contains three components: (1) a summary statement of the current chunk; (2) a transition statement connecting one chunk to the next; and (3) an introductory statement for the next chunk.

> **Summary statement:** We have now learned the seven steps for cleaning the outside of the car.

> **Transition statement:** Now that the outside of the car looks nice, notice how dirty the inside of the car appears.

> **Introduction to next chunk:** Next we will learn six steps for cleaning the inside of a car.

In the past, I've been asked to give specific examples of how bridges work between chunks of content. It is reasonable to place a bridge at the end of a chunk or at the beginning. Here are two examples:

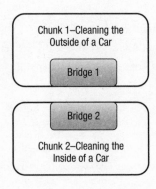

**Bridge 1 content:** We have now learned the seven steps for cleaning the outside of the car. Now that the outside of the car looks nice, notice how dirty the inside of the car appears. In the next segment, we will learn six steps for cleaning the inside of a car.

**Bridge 2 content:** After accomplishing the seven steps to cleaning the outside of the car, it is time to move inside the car. There are six major steps to cleaning the vehicle's interior.

There will be students who move directly from one chunk to the next, but there will also be students who complete one chunk, do something else, and come back to chunk 2 at a later time, so it is helpful to have a short bridge back to the previous content at the beginning.

You are likely to be pressed for time and will not be able to chunk every topic immediately, so you should select the highest-priority items for revision first. Here are some suggestions to consider when you are prioritizing for chunking:

- Items with the most learner questions related to content
- Competency areas for which exam scores are lower
- The most difficult concepts
- Items that prompt the most learner complaints and comments
- Presentations of your own content that bore you (I know, a tough measure!)

In Action Items 39 and 40, you identified chunks and bridges. Now it is time to actually create those chunks. Using your highest-priority items, we'll begin creating content chunks.

**ACTION ITEM 41**

Using a presentation you have already created (perhaps a slide presentation), find the natural breaks in the presentation and divide it into smaller elements approximately 5–7 minutes in length.

**ACTION ITEM 42**

Save these individual chunks using the naming scheme and file and folder structures that you created in Lesson 2, Content Map.

**ACTION ITEM 43**

Add an introduction, activity, and transition to each chunk.

**ACTION ITEM 44**

Repeat Action Items 39–44 for the highest-priority concepts in your course until you have completed these learning experiences for each concept in your course or until you run out of time or until you decide to stop!

After chunking the content for your course, it is now time to set up systems so that you can conveniently capture the information you will need in subsequent semesters. We will establish those systems in Lesson 6, Continuous Improvement.

## FACULTY EXPERIENCES WITH CHUNKING COURSE CONTENT

- A radiography professor realized the benefits of chunking when portions of the content needed to be updated and it took very little time because the presentations were chunked.

- A professional studies professor began chunking course content following student complaints of a recorded lecture that was over an hour.

- A science instructor received positive feedback for a chunked lesson on meiosis. Students benefited from the "repeat-ability" of difficult concepts.

- A faculty development unit received overwhelming response to its chunked learning segments.

Share your ideas on Content and view others in the *Conquering the Content* Community: http://ConqueringtheContent.com/CO/Share

# 6

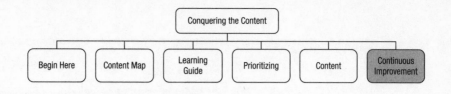

Conquering the Content

| Begin Here | Content Map | Learning Guide | Prioritizing | Content | Continuous Improvement |

# CONTINUOUS IMPROVEMENT

PLAY AUDIO INTRODUCTION ▶  HTTP://CONQUERINGTHECONTENT.COM/CI/INTRO

**Lesson Relevance:** As you teach your online course the first time, you will learn new things that can improve your course for the next time. The systems in this lesson help you capture this information opportunistically throughout the course so that improvements you make are relevant to the challenges you identified during teaching. You can use these techniques term after term to ensure continuous improvement of your online course.

## CONQUERING THE CONTENT: A BLUEPRINT FOR ONLINE COURSE DESIGN AND DEVELOPMENT

Lesson 6, Continuous Improvement

## LEARNING OBJECTIVES

Continuous Improvement

Upon completion of this lesson, you will be able to:

- Create an efficient option for adding to FAQs.
- Log questions that arise and note changes to be made to instructions or other segments of the course.
- Determine due dates for assignments and exams.
- Determine and publicize a schedule of availability for learner support.
- Determine the priority order in which to communicate with learners.
- Develop and save a Communications Log.
- Develop and populate a Link Rot file.
- Communicate your successes to Robin.

135

## LEARNING RESOURCES

References

- Online course
- SoftChalk Lesson Builder (http://softchalk.com/)

## CONTENT

Required Resource

- Smith, R. "Lesson 6, Continuous Improvement." *Conquering the Content: A Blueprint for Online Course Design and Development.* San Francisco: Jossey-Bass, 2014.

## LEARNING ACTIVITIES

Activities for This Lesson

- Determine a consistent schedule of due dates.
- Develop a Course Schedule.
- Determine and publicize your availability.
- Determine priority order in which to communicate with learners.
- Develop and save a Communications Log.
- Develop and populate a Link Rot file.
- Email Robin (robinmsmithphd@gmail.com) to let her know you've *conquered your content* and are ready to teach!

## SELF-ASSESSMENT

Check Your Understanding

- Do you see the advantages to making continuous improvements to your online course?
- Do you have the tracking documents needed to facilitate continuous improvement?

| "Graded" Assessments or Evidence to Proceed | <ul><li>Schedule for the course</li><li>Availability times</li><li>Priority order for communication with learners</li><li>Functional Communications Log</li><li>Functional Link Rot file</li><li>Communication to Robin about your success; email robinsmithphd@gmail.com</li></ul> |
| --- | --- |

Oh my!! Do you need a break? If you are still hanging in there with me, I think it *is* time for a break—how about you? You've done an amazing amount of work, and you probably need to step away for a bit and come back to it more refreshed than you might be at this moment. I have a solution that will mean your course is still progressing while you are taking a much-needed opportunity to focus on something else.

# PEER REVIEW

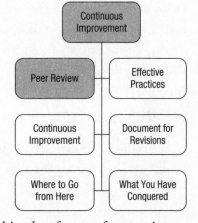

It is now time for you to ask someone else to look over your course materials. If your institution does not have a peer-review process in place, you may want to begin one by informally asking another colleague to review your materials. This idea will eventually catch on.

For a face-to-face course, you and the learners go into the room and shut the door. There is almost no record of what is said in that face-to-face environment except for the notes that learners take. In an online course, in contrast, there is a visible, archived record of what you have presented for the class. This puts online teaching more in line with publishing an article or a chapter in a book than teaching a face-to-face course. Your online course materials are now representing not only you but also your department and your institution. Peer review thus becomes a vitally important part of your course. For example, typographical errors, unclear navigation, out-of-date references, and broken links in your course materials reflect poorly on you, your department, and your institution.

As we've discussed throughout this book, in an online course, the course design becomes much more important than it is in a face-to-face course. You'll need to make a few alterations in your course materials in order to accomplish the same learning outcomes in a very different environment. And as you do, you will have numerous opportunities for teaching in more effective ways.

When I thought in terms of my biology lab, I had the freedom not to worry about spending time getting to each of twenty-five learners to tell them, "No, that is not an *Amoeba*; that is a speck of dust on the cover slip" or "No, that is not *Plasmodium*; that is the pointer in the eyepiece." Instead, I was certain that the images my online learners were seeing were correct.

Many of us think that what happens in the face-to-face environment is sacred and between us and the learners and that, as a bumper sticker I saw stated so eloquently, "What you think of me is none of my business!" However, you have been working on these materials long and hard, and it is difficult at this point to find any errors or typos or even things that may be unclear because you wrote it all and you know what you meant to say. If this is the first time you have offered the course, you may be amazed at the misinterpretations that result. Instructions that seem perfectly clear to you will be misinterpreted in surprising ways.

 **TIME-SAVING TIP**

Request that a friend or colleague unfamiliar with your content help by proofreading your course. He or she will more quickly be able to find small errors you may have missed when concentrating on the big picture. Offer to do the same for a colleague's course.

I promise that you will save time during the semester if you have someone else look over your course now and find all those little issues for you rather than having fifteen to fifty learners each finding and pointing them out during the semester, so that you then have to scramble and find a way to fix them fast.

As I mentioned, an online course is much more like a published article than a lecture you may give. We refer to online content as "enduring material."

Everything is right there in black and white (or bright blue and white) for everyone to see on the screen. You want to present your best work.

While your course is being reviewed, take an opportunity to recognize all the work you have accomplished throughout the last five lessons! Meanwhile, we will set up some systems to ensure that the next time you teach the course, you won't face a large amount of additional work.

**ACTION ITEM 45**

Ask a colleague in your subject matter area to review what you have developed so far. It is important to get feedback prior to placing your content online.

**ACTION ITEM 46**

Take a well-deserved quick break!

# Reflection

It is important for you to create a plan for progression through your course. Once you have all of the content developed, you will need to navigate through your course from the learners' viewpoint. Is it clear how your online course works? What is the overall pace or plan for learners to proceed through the course? Will you have weekly discussions or assignments? What will a typical week be like for your learners? What should they expect as far as time commitment, due dates, and reading time are concerned? Learners should be able to get an idea of the time commitment and frequency of projects, papers, and exams so that they are able to make a plan for working your course into the other aspects of their lives.

The Learning Guides will aid in this structure. An additional element we will add is the Course Schedule. You'll recall that we've made a substantial effort to keep logistical information out of your enduring content so that you may continue to use that content in future semesters. We've placed logistics such as page numbers, dates, and chapter references in the Learning Guides. One additional place to include logistics will be on the Schedule. Before creating the Schedule, there are a few things to keep in mind.

# EFFECTIVE PRACTICES

The following practices have proven effective for multiple faculty members teaching online; you might find them helpful as well.

## Develop a Schedule of Due Dates, and Stick to It

I learned to commit to dates at the beginning of the semester so that learners can arrange work, child care, and other schedules. Showing my learners this respect went a long way toward gaining much cooperation from them. I simply let them know that I understood they were juggling many aspects of their life. I wanted to respect and accommodate that as much as possible and still have education be a priority for them.

## Prioritize a Convenient Schedule

One of the main reasons your learners are taking an online course is for the convenience—not only of not having to commute but also for the scheduling convenience. If we as faculty then require synchronous sessions or frequent tests at monitored sites or tests with very short access time frames, we are negating the very reasons the learners signed up for this course. If there are any time-sensitive requirements, they should be stated prior to enrollment so that learners are not surprised and do not begin the semester feeling they have been misled.

When patients enter medical treatment, they have to sign an informed-consent form. Perhaps it would be helpful if we had something similar in education: a document that informs learners in advance about all the factors in their course and requires consent to those conditions prior to paying tuition.

## Set Due Dates for the Same Day Each Week

It is helpful to learners if they are able to establish a routine with their lives: their families, work schedules, and study routines. If you typically set due dates for the same day of the week throughout the term, this consistency will allow them to establish routines so that they can meet their responsibilities. Allow learners to get into a routine with their assignments and studying. You'll want to keep in mind your availability for answering questions near the due dates.

**ACTION ITEM 47**

Determine a pattern of due dates that will work well with your course. Perhaps elements of the course could be due on Wednesday and Sunday or on Tuesday and Friday.

## Communicate an Appropriate Pace for Working Through the Course

One system I have found helpful is to set due dates in advance. I tell the learners that it is fine for them to work ahead, but they cannot work behind. This is especially important if you use discussion questions in your course. It is not easy to carry on a dynamic discussion with only one other person, and impossible if the learner is the only one in the discussion area during a certain time period because he or she is working ahead or behind the rest of the class members. Even if there is flexible entry and exit, it might be possible to group learners into cohorts based on their entry dates or pace.

The following is an excerpt from a sample schedule. This will give you some ideas for creating your own Course Schedule in the next Action Item 48.

**Biological Sciences Course Schedule**

| Date | Topic | Item | Points |
|------|-------|------|--------|
| Friday, August 21 | Begin Here | Introductions & Syllabus Quiz | 15 pts |
| | | Assignment Submission | 35 pts |
| | | | |
| Monday, August 23 | Ecosystem | Content & Activities | 25 pts |
| Wednesday, August 25 | | Discussion Due | 20 pts |
| Friday, August 27 | | Follow-up Discussion Due | 20 pts |
| | | | |
| | | | |
| | | | |

**ACTION ITEM 48**

Develop a Course Schedule to be located in the Begin Here section of your online course.

**FORM 48**

## COURSE SCHEDULE

| DATE | TOPIC | ITEM | POINTS |
|------|-------|------|--------|
|      |       |      |        |
|      |       |      |        |
|      |       |      |        |
|      |       |      |        |
|      |       |      |        |
|      |       |      |        |
|      |       |      |        |
|      |       |      |        |

Form available at www.josseybass.com/go/conqueringthecontent

# Be Consistent About Navigation

It is helpful to have a course design that is consistent from lesson to lesson so that learners do not have to figure out each time where to go to access content and complete assignments. The course is not a scavenger hunt. It is best to have all the items needed to complete a lesson accessible from one page.

Here is an example, which also demonstrates chunking:

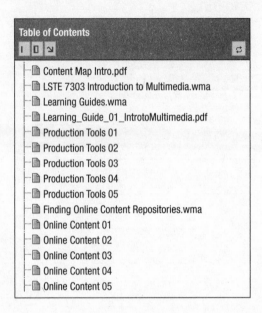

In addition, if you use the Course Outline (Form 7/8) and the Content Map you created earlier to determine the navigation in the course, it has multiple advantages. Your use of the actual content structure as the structure of the course means that every mouse click a learner makes to navigate to a particular topic is reinforcing the scaffolding of the content and helping build that structural element that experts possess. For example, instead of navigating through the course with "noise" (Week 1, Lesson 1, or Chapter 1), learners can select the actual topics. For example, if I had an online course for *Conquering the Content,* you could navigate through my online course selecting "Learning Guide, Learning Activities" to get to the content on activities. That would be more meaningful than "Lesson 3, Section 4."

So that this is less abstract, here are some examples of alignment of the Course Outline, the Content Map, and course navigation based on the first edition of *Conquering the Content.* Notice how all three are the same.

Course Outline:

| Lesson Number/Name | Topic Name |
| --- | --- |
| 1 Design with Learning in Mind | 1 Learning in the 21st Century |
|  | 2 Advantages to Online |
|  | 3 How Online Same as Classroom |
|  | 4 Learning Styles |
|  | 5 Learning vs. Teaching |
|  | 6 Online Environment |
|  | 7 How Online Different than Classroom |
| 2 Design with the Future in Mind | 1 Uncomfortable OK |
|  | 2 Future Here Soon |

Content Map:

Course navigation:

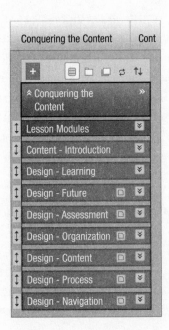

# Navigate to Lesson Components from One Page

It is very helpful if learners are able to navigate to all components of a lesson from one page in the course. All navigation pertaining to Lesson 1 will originate from a single page so that learners are not searching around the learning management system (LMS) for the tasks to be completed. It may make sense to you to group all videos under one icon, all study guides under another, and so on. However, when learners log in to the course to complete a lesson, it is much easier for them to complete what they need to for an individual lesson if everything is on one page. Although you may have everything they need to complete listed in the Learning Guide, it is still important to have tasks grouped on one page so that learners are not spending needless time navigating about the course.

Remember that the Learning Guide includes all the components for a lesson, so you may take the major topics in the Learning Guide and create a table of contents based on this list. Naturally, there will be multiple components of the presentation of content and concepts; these are the chunks you have produced.

Creating the course navigation is so close to the end of the course development process because putting course materials into the LMS before completing those materials will cause extra work. If you have to edit after the files are already in the system, at best you will need to edit outside the LMS and re-upload the files. At worst, you may have to rebuild portions of the course online. There are some easy HTML editors that allow you to preview your lessons with one click of the mouse so that you do not have to move them into an LMS in order to see what they will look like online.

# Be Consistent About Where to Turn In Assignments

The same policy applies here as for navigation. This is all common sense, so I know I needn't say it. It's just that some people get a bit bored with their course design and think that being creative with navigation or assignment submissions or directions will keep the learners on their toes. Learners are more appreciative, though, when your creative energies are put toward making your content exciting, presenting it effectively, and ensuring that they comprehend and remember it.

## Be Consistent About Your Availability

Develop a schedule of times when you will answer questions. Announce that schedule to the class and stick to it. You have to be careful about your own time and schedule. If you have not taught online before, it is tempting to be online seven days a week and to check in as soon as you wake up and just before you go to bed. I did that my first semester of teaching, out of nervousness because I was unsure of how it was all going to work out. I set up unrealistic learner expectations.

One Saturday evening, a learner posted a question at 10:45 p.m., and by 7:00 a.m. the next day (Sunday), I had a nasty message asking why I had not answered the question yet. It really wasn't the learner's fault. All the learners had come to expect me to answer quickly (even though I suspected, and confirmed, that the learner hadn't logged in again between those times) because I had been logging in at those times during the previous three to four weeks. I realized that I wouldn't be sitting in my office between 10:45 p.m. Saturday and 7:00 a.m. Sunday in case a face-to-face learner came by or called my office with a question, and I hadn't suddenly taken on an around-the-clock job, so I shouldn't be so available for the online course either.

I needed to set parameters for learner expectations and for my behavior in regard to when I would take care of my online course. I set times for the learners and myself and determined that I would answer questions posted after 4:00 in the afternoon by approximately 9:00 the next morning. Any questions posted during the day (after 9:00 a.m.) would be answered around 4:00 p.m. The learners therefore knew I would be online Monday through Friday at 9:00 a.m. and 4:00 p.m. and would take care of pending questions at those times. They also knew I would not be online on the weekends, so they needed to be mindful of that schedule and help each other out on the weekends, during the day, and late at night. As long as they knew what to expect, things were fine, and I was also much better off.

## Prioritize and Honor the Order in Which You Will Answer Messages from Learners

Another communication management issue I addressed when I first began teaching online was to prioritize the order in which I would answer messages from learners. My goal is to reach the greatest number of learners.

I also actively tried to minimize communications with individual learners unless it was for personal reasons, for two reasons. First, I did not want to become a personal tutor to twenty-five individual learners, a highly inefficient use of time. Second, I wanted to be sure that all the learners were getting the same information. I was concerned that I would teach one learner something that the other learners would then be missing out on. I had some learners who were too far away to meet with me, and I didn't want someone to have an unfair advantage just because he or she dropped by my office or called.

There are five pathways of communication coming from learners:

- A discussion area or bulletin board where all the learners could see the same information. This is the most efficient because everyone in the class sees it.

- Email within the course. This is the next most efficient, because I choose when I get to read it.

- Email to my university account. This inserts itself among hundreds of other emails and has a tendency to get lost in the shuffle. Receiving learner emails here also means that I don't have all course correspondence in one place.

- Telephone calls. These are fine for making appointments for assistance or in an emergency situation. Some instructors prefer this method of contact from participants in their course.

- Text messages. Will you accept these? If so, what times of the day or night?

This is the priority sequence I announce to the learners, and I have trained myself to be diligent in following it:

*Discussion area.* I explain that this is the quickest way to get in touch with me and that I always answer these questions first. So when I log in at 9:00 a.m. and 4:00 p.m., I go straight to the discussion area or bulletin board and answer those questions. I select the discussion area first because it is the quickest way to reach the greatest number of learners. Everyone in the class has the opportunity to access the information in this area.

*Messaging or email within the course.* After answering all the questions in the discussion area, I check the course messages. If any of the questions in the messages pertain to content, I reply to the sender saying that I received the message and think the question is of interest to the entire class. I post the answer to the question in the discussion area/bulletin board, and I reference the subject line of the message. In this way, I redirect the learners to the discussion area, pointing out that it is the place to get information about the course. I answer only personal or grade questions in messaging or email—that is, the types of personal questions one would answer during office hours.

*Email to my work account.* I tell learners that the only email they should send to my office account is for something of a technical nature (if something is wrong with the server or the course) or if there is a personal problem. If they are asking for course information, I reply to the email asking them to log in to the course and send this message as a discussion area message or an email message, whichever is appropriate; I also refer them to the course syllabus, which gives those directions. In addition, I will not reply to that email until after I have answered all the messages in the discussion area and the course emails.

*Telephone calls.* These are almost always of a personal nature. If a call is not personal, I ask the learner to first post the message on the bulletin board. If the learner has already done this and is still having difficulty with the concept, then certainly a telephone call is in order. I even call the learner later if this person indicates that he or she is still having difficulty. I also inquire about the materials in the course and find out what wasn't clear and what might be helpful to make it clear to the learner.

These rules for prioritization of communication are more for me than the learners. Nevertheless, the learners adhere to them much better than I do. I want to jump every time one of them has a question, but I have to remember that sometimes they figure it out on their own and sometimes they help each other figure it out, and these ways of learning are much better than my telling them.

I remember at the end of my master's program thanking my major professor for not being there every time I went down the hall to find him to answer a question. I was stuck and needed help, but when he wasn't there, I went back and struggled more and eventually worked many things out on my own. I think there are times when our learners might benefit from a few chances to struggle with the content for a little while.

Now it's your turn, Action Item 50 asks you to determine the priority order in which you would like to respond to learner questions.

**ACTION ITEM 50**

Communicate the priority order in which you will respond to communication.

# CONTINUOUS IMPROVEMENT

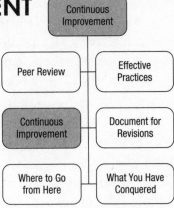

You will be making revisions to your course in the future. If you've followed the system in this book, everything is well formatted for you to make those revisions easily. During the first semester you teach, you will notice portions of the course that don't work the way you envisioned. This is to be expected, so don't be dismayed when this occurs. Perhaps what I wrote didn't come across to you exactly as I meant it, or perhaps your teaching style or your course materials are a bit different or you have a unique set of learners with different needs. Any of these conditions will require you to customize your individual courses to fit your needs. Further, your institution has its own unique policies, regulations, or politics that you need to follow in order for you to blend into your environment.

I will suggest several documents for you to keep at hand so that you can be opportunistic about keeping records of your observations. Then when it is time to update your course, you will have all the information you need in one place.

The Communications Log is the most comprehensive of these documents; it allows you to develop course revisions based on learning outcomes and learner need. You may not have time to revise everything you want to after the first semester of teaching, so it is important to prioritize these revisions based on the goal of increasing performance on learning outcomes.

To aid in prioritizing revisions to your course, you can document requests for assistance on the Communications Log sequentially as requests or concerns arise. There are multiple purposes for documenting these requests. First, you note the number of learner requests you are receiving. With this information documented, you are equipped to show your supervisor the volume of learner interactions in which you are involved even though you are not "meeting a class"; track "high maintenance" learners (those learners who require an inordinate amount of your time, register late, request make-up exams, miss deadlines, and just don't have it all together yet); and ascertain how learners fare in your course relative to their computer and reading skills.

Second, the Communications Log points to portions of the course in which issues occur that are due to students' preferred learning styles. Log the learning styles of learners and the portions of the course where issues occur; the frequency of requests from individual learners; and the time on task required for you to address concerns about particular portions of your online course. From this information, you can determine whether the issues are logistical and related to a need for clarification of directions or processes and for increased computer skills, or concept related, requiring you to clarify concepts, provide background information, or offer additional learning exercises. The Communications Log will also reveal whether visual, auditory, kinesthetic, read-write, or global explanations in your course are lacking, depending on the frequency of requests from learners with these preferred learning styles in each component of your course.

With the Communications Log, you can track the amount of time you are spending during the semester solving problems in your course. As mentioned, you also can track "high-maintenance" learners. Documentation can help you discover whether your interventions with them are making a difference or whether these learners taking an inordinate amount of your time eventually drop and prove to be a drain on the time you have available to spend with other learners who progress through the course. Check for correlations between these learners and learners who enrolled late but within institutional deadlines, who were allowed to bend the rules on prerequisites for entry into your course, who do not have a computer at home, or who were allowed to enter the course beyond normal institutional enrollment deadlines; also compare learners in each of these situations compared to those who eventually drop the course. The Communications Log is in the format of a spreadsheet or word processing table that lists several columns of information.

Create a Communications Log to capture issues, suggestions, and questions from learners.

## COMMUNICATIONS LOG

Course Name _____ Term Dates _____

| DATE | NAME | TOPIC | LESSON | QUESTION | NOTES |
|------|------|-------|--------|----------|-------|
|      |      |       |        |          |       |
|      |      |       |        |          |       |
|      |      |       |        |          |       |
|      |      |       |        |          |       |
|      |      |       |        |          |       |
|      |      |       |        |          |       |
|      |      |       |        |          |       |
|      |      |       |        |          |       |
|      |      |       |        |          |       |
|      |      |       |        |          |       |
|      |      |       |        |          |       |
|      |      |       |        |          |       |

Form available at www.josseybass.com/go/conqueringthecontent

# DOCUMENT FOR REVISIONS

During each semester of your online course, keep a record of the issues that will need attention in your course prior to the next time it is taught. It is much easier to note these along the way than to try to think back through it all during the busyness of the next semester. Here are the categories I've found helpful in updating courses.

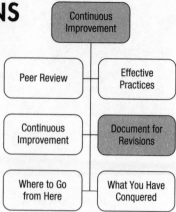

## FAQs

Keeping a list of FAQs for your course is a way to reduce your time on task yet still provide answers to learners' questions. You may want to have two FAQ lists: one on course procedures and another on content. I typically post the FAQs in the Begin Here section of the course. You may update these documents as the need arises. I've found it helpful to make an announcement of any new FAQ answers in the discussion area when I first compose them. If a question was not in the list of FAQs at the beginning of the course, then I add it to the FAQ file, and it will be available from that point forward, including the beginning of the next semester. You can gather much of this from the Communications Log, or keep a separate document that you update in your online course.

## List of Issues and Revisions

As issues arise during the semester, you'll find it convenient to compile them in one file. As you record each issue, if you have an idea about how to revise the course to alleviate this concern, record it alongside the issue. With these issues and ideas gathered in one place, it will be much more efficient for you to make the changes to improve your course for the following semester. Again, the Communications Log can fulfill this purpose, or make it a separate document if you prefer.

# Suggestions

During your course, learners may make suggestions about it. Do not view these suggestions as criticism; rather, they are sources of useful information for you. I usually tell learners when they are the pioneers for the online version of the course or for a new element of design within the course, and say that any suggestions they make about the course will be welcome and can benefit learners who take the course in the future.

Learners have a unique perspective on your course that you cannot duplicate, no matter how many times you review the course. One of your goals is for your course to be as effective as possible, and learners can go a long way toward assisting you with this goal. I've found that learners are eager to help and usually provide valuable input for making course revisions. You may have to distinguish between comments that are attempts to increase grades and comments that are truly constructive, but you will most likely be able to recognize the difference. Asking for suggestions provides an additional opportunity for you to show respect to your learners, which in turn typically garners a favorable view of you as an instructor.

# Blog or Journal of Your Experiences

It is to my great regret that I did not write my experiences in a journal the first few semesters I taught online. I did several comparisons between online and face-to-face courses during my first four to six semesters of teaching. A record of my own observations during the experience would have been valuable to me now.

One experience I remember well is when I taught both an online course and a face-to-face course at the same time. I gave both groups of learners access to both modes of delivery. I thought that the online learners would want to come to class in order to see real-time demonstrations and have an opportunity to get the information in person. To my great surprise, it was the face-to-face learners who wanted access to the online materials, and not a single learner taking the online course ever came to a face-to-face session. I suppose I could have seen this as an indictment of my teaching presence, but my optimistic outlook led me to conclude that it was due to the value and convenience of the online materials. In fact, this view was supported by learner evaluations of the courses at the end of the semester. I mentioned earlier my realization that use of the Learning Guides online and the experience of revising my course organization as a whole changed my face-to-face teaching for the better.

I am certain there were many other valuable experiences that could have provided similar insights had I taken the time to record them. It is common among faculty teaching online to undergo experiences valuable to their teaching. Evidence of these experiences in a journal will serve as a record of your growth as an instructor and can benefit those of us who are continuously learning from the sharing of one another's teaching experiences. A blog or journal may become an entry in your teaching portfolio and can also give you important insights about teaching and learning as your skills progress. It may surprise you how much your teaching skills are advanced by the experience of teaching an online course. And what teacher doesn't benefit from a positive achievement?

## Items to Document

It is beneficial to prepare for course revisions and updates during the first semester you teach your online course. Once again, it will be important for you to prioritize the revisions to be made before teaching your course for the second time. The highest-priority revisions will be those that have an effect on learner outcomes. Documenting the following items will assist in your determining the priority revision:

- Concepts that were difficult, or test or assignment questions that caused difficulty
- Discussion questions that needed clarification
- Assignments that needed more explicit instructions, alterations, or changes to grading
- Assignment rubrics that have not worked well

- Quiz questions with issues—for example, poor wording or answer choices or incorrect number of points assigned
- Project feedback from learners
- Updates for presentations of text-based content
- Updates of content in response to current events

If you have feedback you give frequently for assignments, consider keeping a file of these explanations so that you can copy and paste without having to recreate this information each time. An example might be an explanation on the use of adverbs and adjectives for written papers.

This list seems like a lot to document, but it can be easy to maintain. I keep a file on my desktop to record this information so that with one mouse click, I am into the file and typing my ideas.

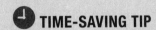

**TIME-SAVING TIP**

Reduce mouse clicks wherever possible. Save files you will access frequently directly onto your desktop so that they are easily accessible with one mouse click. Files useful to keep on your desktop may include your FAQs list, learner questions, and your revisions list for the course.

# Link Rot

Link rot is just what it sounds like, and when your links rot, you need to know! Websites might move or be reorganized, so you need a system to check those links periodically. Typically links will be scattered throughout your course at the places where learners need to access them. You don't want to alter the course design that enables learners to have all their materials where they need them, but it is not efficient for you to go through the entire course page by page searching for links to check. It is also not very professional to wait until the link breaks and let the learners tell you there are rotten links in your course.

I have an efficient and convenient way of ensuring that your course does not become infested with link rot. Paste every link in the course (preferably as you create each) into the Link Rot Form and also note the location of the link within the topic and lesson element. Then once a month or so, open the spreadsheet and click on each URL to find out if it is still working. For any that are no longer current, find the updated link, log it on the form, and then go directly to the course content where it is listed and replace the URL.

**FORM 52**

## LINK ROT FORM

Course Name _____  Last Updated _____

| URL | TOPIC | LESSON ELEMENT | LOCATION |
| --- | --- | --- | --- |
|  |  |  |  |
|  |  |  |  |
|  |  |  |  |
|  |  |  |  |
|  |  |  |  |
|  |  |  |  |
|  |  |  |  |
|  |  |  |  |
|  |  |  |  |

Form available at www.josseybass.com/go/conqueringthecontent

# WHERE TO GO FROM HERE

In spite of all the information in this book, there is still more to learn. Two topics are of major interest: the LMS and facilitating an online course.

## Learning Management System (LMS)

One of the things you will need to tackle is getting your content into your LMS or onto a website. Regardless of which delivery method your institution is using, you will need to find out how to access the course you will be developing. Make friends with those who are responsible for support and instructional design at your institution. These relationships will be invaluable.

Course delivery works in different ways on different campuses, so you'll have to find the appropriate person to talk with at your institution and request any access that needs to be granted. Some institutions expect the faculty to upload course materials themselves; others have people who input the course materials for the faculty (this is less common). If you need to develop the course yourself, you may be required to go through a training or certification course before you are allowed to teach with that system. Therefore, investigate the policies on your campus for online learning faculty.

## Facilitating an Online Course

In this lesson, I addressed managing learner communication and other issues that will come into play as you are teaching. I did not fully address facilitating group discussions, collaborative learning, or group work; you will want to learn more about these sorts of issues, depending on the way you will be running your course. I suggest consulting several good references; the following are some examples:

Conrad, R., and Donaldson, J. *Continuing to Engage the Online Learner: More Activities and Resources for Creative Instruction.* San Francisco: Jossey-Bass, 2012.

Palloff, R., and Pratt, K. *Collaborating Online: Learning Together in Community.* San Francisco: Jossey-Bass, 2004.

Palloff, R., and Pratt, K. *Building Online Communities: Effective Strategies for the Virtual Classroom.* San Francisco: Jossey-Bass, 2007.

Weimer, M. *Learner-Centered Teaching: Five Key Changes to Practice.* San Francisco: Jossey-Bass, 2002.

# WHAT YOU HAVE CONQUERED

Wow! Take a look at how far you've come since you started this book. You have accomplished a tremendous amount and should be pleased with your progress! After classes begin, you will be relieved that you have put in this much preparation time in advance of the start of the semester.

| Continuous Improvement | |
| --- | --- |
| Peer Review | Effective Practices |
| Continuous Improvement | Document for Revisions |
| Where to Go from Here | What You Have Conquered |

Now take an opportunity to congratulate yourself and celebrate your accomplishments. If you are still reading at this point, you are definitely a conqueror!

Thank you for making the journey with me. I would love to know about the course you have developed or are in the process of developing. Please send me a quick email and let me know you made it to the end of the book and what subject matter you are teaching. I am interested in knowing how *Conquering the Content: A Blueprint for Online Course Design and Development* worked for you and what challenges you are experiencing.

## FACULTY EXPERIENCES WITH CONTINUOUS IMPROVEMENT

- A pharmacy professor noticed improvements in a colleague's online courses after asking that person to review his own course.

- Use of a Communications Log elucidated a pattern of questions on a particular biology assignment, which allowed the professor to efficiently target areas of needed improvement in his course.

- Faculty assistance for placing a course online was suddenly available for one week at a community college; those faculty who had used a naming scheme for files and folders were able to quickly accept the assistance.

**SHARE**

Share your Continuous Improvement ideas and view others in the *Conquering the Content* Community: http://ConqueringtheContent.com/CI/Share

**ACTION ITEM 53**

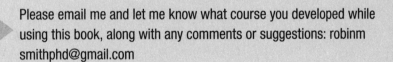

Please email me and let me know what course you developed while using this book, along with any comments or suggestions: robinm smithphd@gmail.com

I look forward to hearing from you!

## Congratulations on Conquering the Content!

# REFERENCES

Ambrose, S., Bridges, M., DiPietro, M., Lovett, M., and Norman, M. *How Learning Works: 7 Research-Based Principles for Smart Teaching.* San Francisco: Jossey-Bass, 2010.

American Association of Higher Education Assessment Forum. *Nine Principles of Good Practice for Assessing Student Learning,* 1996. http://www.academicprograms.calpoly.edu/pdfs/assess/nine_principles_good_practice.pdf

Anderson, L. W. (ed.), Krathwohl, D. R. (ed.), Airasian, P.W., Cruikshank, K. A., Mayer, R. E., Pintrich, P. R., Rather, J., and Wittrock, M. C. *A Taxonomy for Learning, Teaching, and Assessing: A Revision of Bloom's Taxonomy of Educational Objectives.* New York: Longman, 2001.

Awalt, C. "Speaking Personally—with Tony Bates." *American Journal of Distance Education,* 2007, *21*(2), 105–109.

Boettcher, J. "Ten Core Principles for Designing Effective Learning Environments: Insights from Brain Research and Pedagogical Theory." *Innovate,* 2007, *3*(3). http://www.Innovateonline.info/index.php?viewarticle&id54

Chandler, P., and Sweller, J. "The Split-Attention Effect as a Factor in the Design of Instruction." *British Journal of Educational Psychology,* 1992, *62*(2), 233–246.

Chickering, A., and Ehrmann, S. "Implementing the Seven Principles: Technology as Lever." *AAHE Bulletin,* October 1996, pp. 3–6.

Chickering, A., and Gamson, Z. "Seven Principles for Good Practice in Undergraduate Education." *AAHE Bulletin,* March 1987, pp. 3–6.

Clark, R. C., Nguyen, F., and Sweller, J. *Efficiency in Learning: Evidence-Based Guidelines to Manage Cognitive Load.* San Francisco: Jossey-Bass/Pfeiffer, 2006.

Comeaux, P. *Assessing Online Learning.* San Francisco: Jossey-Bass, 2005.

Conrad, R., and Donaldson, J. *Continuing to Engage the Online Learner: More Activities and Resources for Creative Instruction.* San Francisco: Jossey-Bass, 2012.

Cook, M. P. "Visual Representations in Science Education: The Influence of Prior Knowledge and Cognitive Load Theory on Instructional Design Principles." *Science Education,* 2006, *90*(6), 1073–1091.

Draves, W. A. *Teaching Online* (2nd ed.). River Falls, Wis.: Learning Resources Network, 2002.

Dweck, C. *Mindset: The New Psychology of Success, How We Can Learn to Fulfill Our Potential.* New York: Ballantine Books, 2006.

Felder, R. "Learning and Teaching Styles in Engineering Education." *Engineering Education,* 1988, 78(7), 674–681.

Felder, R. "Reaching the Second Tier: Learning and Teaching Styles in College Science Education." *Journal of College Science Teaching,* 1993, *23*(5), 286–290.

Felder, R. M., and Soloman, B. A. (n.d.). "Index of Learning Styles." Accessed May 23, 2014. http://www.ncsu.edu/felder-public/ILSpage.html

Finkelstein, J. *Learning in Real Time: Synchronous Teaching and Learning Online.* San Francisco: Jossey-Bass, 2006.

Garrison, D., Anderson, T., and Archer, W. "Critical Thinking, Cognitive Presence and Computing Conferencing in Distance Education." *American Journal of Distance Education,* 2001, *15*(1), 7–23.

Horton, W. *E-Learning by Design* (2nd ed.). San Francisco: Pfeiffer/Wiley, 2012.

Kalyuga, S., Chandler, P., and Sweller, J. "Managing Split-Attention and Redundancy in Multimedia Instruction." *Applied Cognitive Psychology*, 1999, *13*(4), 351–371.

Kruse, K. "Designing eLearning User Interfaces Part 1: Assisting User Memory—Brain Memory." 2005. http://www.e-learningguru.com/articles /art4_2.htm

Lehman, R. M., and Conceição, S.C.O. *Creating a Sense of Presence in Online Teaching: How to "Be There" for Distance Learners.* San Francisco: Jossey-Bass, 2010.

Mayer, R. E. *Multimedia Learning* (2nd ed.). New York: Cambridge University Press, 2009.

Marsh, R., Sebrechts, M., Hicks, J., and Landau, J. "Processing Strategies and Secondary Memory in Very Rapid Forgetting." *Memory and Cognition*, 1997, *25*, 174–181.

Merrill, M. "First Principles of Instruction." *Educational Technology Research and Development*, 2002, *50*(3), 43–59.

Miller, G. "The Magical Number Seven, Plus or Minus Two: Some Limits on Our Capacity for Processing Information." *Psychological Review*, 1956, *63*, 81–97.

Moreno, R. "Animated Pedagogical Agents in Educational Technology." *Educational Technology*, 2004, *44*(6), 23–30.

Nilson, L. B. *The Graphical Syllabus and the Outcomes Map: Communicating Your Course.* San Francisco: Jossey-Bass, 2007.

Palloff, R., and Pratt, K. *Collaborating Online: Learning Together in Community.* San Francisco: Jossey-Bass, 2004.

Palloff, R., and Pratt, K. *Building Online Communities: Effective Strategies for the Virtual Classroom.* San Francisco: Jossey-Bass, 2007.

Pomales-Garcia, C., and Liu, Y. "Web-Based Distance Learning Technology: The Impacts of Web Modules' Length and Format." *American Journal of Distance Education*, 2006, *20*(3), 163–179.

Reiser, R. A., and Dempsey, J. V. *Trends and Issues in Instructional Design and Technology* (3rd ed.). Boston: Pearson Education, 2012.

Steen, R. *The Evolving Brain: The Known and the Unknown.* Amherst, N.Y.: Prometheus Books, 2007.

Tobias, S. *They're Not Dumb, They're Different: Stalking the Second Tier.* Washington, D.C.: Science News Books, 1991.

Walvoord, B. E., and Anderson, V. J. *Effective Grading: A Tool for Learning and Assessment.* San Francisco: Jossey-Bass, 1998.

Weimer, M. *Learner-Centered Teaching: Five Key Changes to Practice.* San Francisco: Jossey-Bass, 2002.

Wlodkowski, R. J., and Ginsberg, M. B. *Teaching Intensive and Accelerated Courses: Instruction That Motivates Learning.* San Francisco: Jossey-Bass, 2010.

Wu, H. K., and Shah, P. "Exploring Visuospatial Thinking in Chemistry Learning." *Science Education*, 2004, *88*, 465–492.

# GLOSSARY

**Alignment**   Refers to the coordination of objectives, content, learning activities, and assessments.

**Authentic assessment**   Assessment that models a real-world environment or reality-based application of concepts. For example, if an assessment is based on demonstrating the correct structure of a paragraph, writing a paragraph would be an authentic assessment. Answering multiple-choice questions about the correct structure of a paragraph would not be considered an authentic assessment.

**Begin Here**   Component of an online course that includes specific information about how the course works, the pace of learning, and channels of communication. Often includes a video or audio introduction from the faculty member.

**Chunk-ability**   A quality which describes content that can be conveniently accessed in small segments as the learner has time.

**Chunking**   Dividing content into absorbable segments; example: 5- to 7-minute segments of content.

**Communications Log**   A record of communications from learners that assists the faculty member/subject matter expert in evaluating the highest-priority items for course revision.

**Content Map**   A graphical representation of the overview and relationship of topics and subtopics within a course.

**Course delivery**   That activity of facilitating the course that occurs during the actual offering of the course. Contrast with *Course design* and *Course development*.

**Course design**   The early plan or blueprint of a course that will be used to develop and later deliver the online course. The course design is often facilitated by an instructional designer. A template might also be part of a coherent course design.

**Course development**   Those activities associated with preparing course content prior to course delivery.

**Learning Guide**   A (typically) one-page document to guide student learning through a lesson. Also serves as a course development map for faculty/subject matter experts. The Learning Guide is developed in advance of the remainder of the course content and aids in prioritizing course development.

**Link rot**   Broken links within a course resulting from external links that have been changed.

**Lesson**   May also be termed "module." A segment of content that contains a lesson introduction, a lesson relevance section, a Learning Guide, content, a self-assessment, and a lesson assessment.

**Lesson introduction**   An audio or video introduction to the lesson.

**Lesson relevance**   A statement that helps learners see how the lesson relates to their current environment or to the entire course or program.

**LMS**   Learning management system—system used to deliver course content to learners.

**Module**   *See Lesson.*

**Pause-ability**   A quality which describes content that is formatted in such a way that it may be paused while in progress and later resumed without having to revert to the beginning.

**Repeat-ability**   A quality which describes content that is formatted in such a way that learners may review it multiple times.

**SME**   Subject matter expert/faculty member; SMEs often partner with instructional designers, graphic artists, and others to help develop a robust online course.

**Understand-ability**   A quality which describes content that is easily comprehensible to learners.

## ACTION ITEMS

## Lesson 1: Begin Here

**ACTION ITEM 1**

Think of your favorite teacher from all your years of school—the one who made a positive lasting impression on you.

Using Form 1, document the qualities that stood out about this person.

**ACTION ITEM 2**

Brainstorm for a few minutes about the added value you as a unique individual bring to your course.

**ACTION ITEM 3**

Select one course on which to focus as you work through the process outlined in this book.

Gather all materials associated with the selected course, including syllabus, schedule, objectives, assignments, quizzes, book, feedback from student evaluations of teaching, and so on.

Document current course organization and the benefits or challenges of individual lessons.

## Lesson 2: Content Map

Translate chapter numbers into topic names using Form 6.

Record the five to seven highest-priority subtopics for each lesson. Repeat this step for each of the topics in your course.

**ACTION ITEM 8**

Select five to seven sub-subtopics within which to organize the content for each subtopic and record these. Repeat this step for each of the subtopics in your course.

**ACTION ITEM 9**

Decide on a format to use for your Content Map.

**ACTION ITEM 10**

Using the outline you created, add topics to the Content Map format of your choice.

**ACTION ITEM 11**

Review and revise the Content Map you have created. The Action Items for the remainder of this lesson will be based on your final Content Map.

ACTION ITEM 12

Make a folder for one lesson in your own storage area or on your storage device (not in the LMS).

ACTION ITEM 13

Make a subfolder within the folder you made in Action Item 12 for each component of the Learning Guide for which you will have multiple files—for example:

ContentL01

LearningResourcesL01

AssignmentsL01

Again, label each of these subfolders so you will know it belongs to Lesson01. Place all folders and subfolders in your own storage area.

ACTION ITEM 14

Copy the folder and subfolder structure you just created, and paste it into the main course folder enough times to have a set of folders and subfolders for each of your lessons.

**ACTION ITEM 15**

Rename the new folders according to the lesson number. Use leading zeroes and number the folders for lessons below the number 10 (for example, Lesson01, Lesson02). These will be the names you see in the filing system, but in the areas where learners are able to view the names (this will be inside the LMS), it is more helpful to use topic names.

## Lesson 3: Learning Guide

**ACTION ITEM 16**

Download the Learning Guide Blueprint from http://Conqueringthe Content.com.

**ACTION ITEM 17**

Customize the Learning Guide Blueprint or develop a format of your own to use.

**ACTION ITEM 18**

Using the Content Map and file-naming scheme you developed in Lesson 2, create one Learning Guide file for each topic.

**ACTION ITEM 19**

Save each of these files with the file-naming scheme you developed in Lesson 2 (perhaps LG01TopicName, LG02TopicName, and so on).

**ACTION ITEM 20**

Determine the dates that each lesson will be covered and record those at the top of the Learning Guide for each lesson.

**ACTION ITEM 21**

Record the course title and lesson topic on each Learning Guide.

**ACTION ITEM 22**

Create a small image of the Content Map showing the particular lesson highlighted or with a different shape.

**ACTION ITEM 23**

Develop objectives or outcomes for each lesson, and record them in the appropriate Learning Guide.

**ACTION ITEM 24**

Brainstorm for a moment and record the best way for a person to learn the first objective you just developed.

**ACTION ITEM 25**

Repeat Action Item 24 for each of the objectives of the lessons of your course.

**ACTION ITEM 26**

Identify references or resources your learners will need to complete each lesson and record those in the appropriate Learning Guide.

**ACTION ITEM 27**

Distinguish between required resources and supplemental resources so that it is clear where learners need to focus their attention.

**ACTION ITEM 28**

Reserve or find links to resources that you have referenced in the "Tools to Help Me Learn" section.

**ACTION ITEM 29**

Identify learning activities and assignments you will have for learners for each lesson and record these in the appropriate Learning Guide.

**ACTION ITEM 30**

Develop detailed directions for each assignment and learning activity so that learners know exactly where to turn in or submit evidence of their learning. Include specific identifier information (file name, subject heading, and any other information you prefer) that the learner needs in order to submit work. Determine the dates and times that assignments will be due.

**ACTION ITEM 31**

Develop self-assessments for each lesson and record them in the appropriate Learning Guide.

**ACTION ITEM 32**

Plan assessments for the learning objectives and activities for each lesson.

**ACTION ITEM 33**

Create the assessment activities for each lesson.

# Lesson 4: Prioritizing

ACTION ITEM 34

Rank, in priority order, the items yet to be developed that you think will have the greatest impact on your students.

I-1.

I-2.

I-3.

I-4.

I-5.

I-6.

I-7.

I-8.

I-9.

I-10.

Rank, in priority order, the items yet to be developed that you think will take the least amount of time to develop.

T-1.

T-2.

T-3.

T-4.

T-5.

T-6.

T-7.

T-8.

T-9.

T-10.

Plot the items from the two lists you created in Action Items 34 and 35 into the four quadrants.

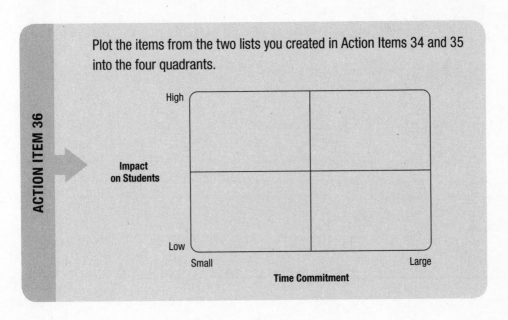

Rank, in priority order, how you want to proceed (I-1, T-1, I-2, T-2).

1.

2.

3.

4.

5.

6.

7.

8.

9.

10.

|  | Small | Large |
|---|---|---|
| High | 1 | 2/3 |
| Impact on Students | | |
| Low | 3/2 | 4 |

Time Commitment

# Lesson 5: Content

ACTION ITEM 38

Take Felder and Soloman's Index of Learning Styles Questionnaire (http://www.engr.ncsu.edu/learningstyles/ilsweb.html) and record your scores along the continua.

| Perceiving | 11 | 9 | 7 | 5 | 3 | 1 | 1 | 3 | 5 | 7 | 9 | 11 | Intuitive |
|---|---|---|---|---|---|---|---|---|---|---|---|---|---|
| Visual | 11 | 9 | 7 | 5 | 3 | 1 | 1 | 3 | 5 | 7 | 9 | 11 | Auditory |
| Active | 11 | 9 | 7 | 5 | 3 | 1 | 1 | 3 | 5 | 7 | 9 | 11 | Reflective |
| Sequential | 11 | 9 | 7 | 5 | 3 | 1 | 1 | 3 | 5 | 7 | 9 | 11 | Global |

ACTION ITEM 39

Using your Content Map as a guide, identify concepts to be used as chunks for one of your lessons.

ACTION ITEM 40

Identify introduction, content chunks, learning activities, and bridges for one of your lessons.

**ACTION ITEM 41**

Using a presentation you have already created (perhaps a slide presentation), find the natural breaks in the presentation and divide it into smaller elements approximately 5–7 minutes in length.

**ACTION ITEM 42**

Save these individual chunks using the naming scheme and file and folder structures that you created in Lesson 2, Content Map.

**ACTION ITEM 43**

Add an introduction, activity, and transition to each chunk.

**ACTION ITEM 44**

Repeat Action Items 39–44 for the highest-priority concepts in your course until you have completed these learning experiences for each concept in your course or until you run out of time or until you decide to stop!

# Lesson 6: Continuous Improvement

**ACTION ITEM 45**

Ask a colleague in your subject matter area to review what you have developed so far. It is important to get feedback prior to placing your content online.

**ACTION ITEM 46**

Take a well-deserved quick break!

**ACTION ITEM 47**

Determine a pattern of due dates that will work well with your course. Perhaps elements of the course could be due on Wednesday and Sunday or on Tuesday and Friday.

**ACTION ITEM 48**

Develop a Course Schedule to be located in the Begin Here section of your online course.

**ACTION ITEM 49**

Develop a schedule of availability and provide this information in your online course.

**ACTION ITEM 50**

Communicate the priority order in which you will respond to communication.

**ACTION ITEM 51**

Create a Communications Log to capture issues, suggestions, and questions from learners.

**ACTION ITEM 52**

Create a Link Rot Form with all links from your course in one place so that you can easily check and update them.

Please email me and let me know what course you developed while using this book, along with any comments or suggestions: robinm smithphd@gmail.com

# INDEX

Learning online, *See* Online learning

Learning phases, 5

Learning resources: connections, making, 74–75; gathering, 74; lesson assessment, 82–85; self-assessments, 81–82

Learning styles, 108–112

Lehman, R. M., 18

Lesson assessment, 82–85; advance planning, 83; authentic assessments, 83–84; quizzes, 84–85

Lesson introduction, 168

Lesson (module), 47, 104, 125, 168

Link rot, 157–158, 168; defined, 157; form, 158

Liu, Y., 118, 125

Lovett, M., xviii

## M

Marsh, R., 78

Mayer, R. E., xviii, 41, 71

Merrill, M., 2, 5, 79

Miller, G., 122, 125

Modality principle, 118

Module, *See* Lesson (module)

Moreno, R., 81

*Multimedia Learning* (Mayer), 41–42

My Favorite Teacher (form), 4

## N

Naming schemes, 49

Navigating to lesson components, 146

Navigation, consistency about, 143–145

New tools, timing the introduction of, 11

Nguyen, F., 107, 112, 114, 116, 118

Nilson, L. B., 30

"No books" policy, 24

Nonenduring elements, defined, 58

Norman, M., xviii

## O

Online content: chunk-ability, 115; pause-ability, 116; qualities of, 115–117; repeat-ability, 115–116; understand-ability, 116

Online course: advantages of, 12–13; facilitating, 159–160

Online learning, 7–10: advantages of, 12–13; course content characteristics, 17; course design/development vs. course delivery/facilitation, 18–19; course documentation, 21–22; course selection, 20–22; environment, 13–14; face-to-face learning vs., 16–20; faculty member's role, 17–18; first-time online instructors, 23–28; future updates, current preparation for, 19–20; learner's role, 16–17; pace, 10; place, 9; time, 9; two-minute test, 14; visual cues, lack of, 16

## P

Palloff, R., 18, 160

Pause-ability, 115, 116, 118–119, 168; defined, 17

Peer review, 137–140

Pintrich, P. R., 71

Points: balancing effort and, 25; earned, 85–86

Pomales-Garcia, C., 118, 125

Pratt, K., 18, 125, 160

Presentation length, 118–119

Presentation of information, 119

Prior learning, organization of, 112–114

Prioritizing, 89–105; action items, 180–182; course development, 90–92; faculty anxiety, reducing, 96–97; faculty experiences with, 102; learner anxiety, reducing, 92–93; learner needs, 93–95; priorities blueprint, selecting, 98–102; teaching for the long term, 102–105

## Q

Quizzes, 84–85

## R

Rather, J., 71

Reflection, 139–140

Reiser, R. A., 116

Repeat-ability, 115–116, 118–119, 168; defined, 17

# If you enjoyed this book, you may also like these:

**Motivating and Retaining Online Students:**
**Research-Based Strategies That Work**
**by Rosemary M. Lehman,**
**Simone C.O. Conceição**
ISBN: 9781118531709

**Continuing to Engage the Online Learner:**
**More Activities and Resources**
**for Creative Instruction**
**by Rita-Marie Conrad, J. Ana Donaldson**
ISBN: 9781118000175

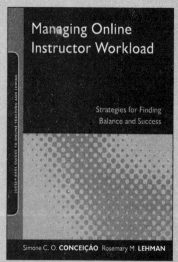

**Managing Online Instructor Workload:**
**Strategies for Finding Balance and Success**
**by Simone C.O. Conceição, Rosemary M. Lehman**
ISBN: 9780470888421

**Assessing the Online Learner:**
**Resources and Strategies for Faculty**
**by Rena M. Palloff, Keith Pratt**
ISBN: 9780470283868